The Race For The 21ST Century

by

TIM LAHAYE

THOMAS NELSON PUBLISHERS
Nashville • Camden • New York

Published in Nashville, Tennessee, by Thomas Nelson, Inc. and distributed in Canada by Lawson Falle, Ltd., Cambridge, Ontario.

Printed in the United States of America.

Library of Congress Cataloging-in-Publication Data

LaHaye, Tim F.
The Race for the 21st century

   Bibliography: p.
   1. Sociology, Christian.   2. Twenty-first century—
Forecasts.   I. Title.
BT738.L24   1986   303.4'9'09048   86-19339
ISBN 0-8407-7757-4 (pbk.)

Contents

STEP FOUR:
PREPARE YOURSELF AND YOUR FAMILY

Preface

Few people realize that we have just lived through the most rapid rate of change in the history of the world—1956 to 1986—and that the next thirty years will make the past thirty obsolete. A statement by Congressman Newt Gingrich puts the current rate of accelerated change in perspective. When you realize that "the entire first flight of the Wright brothers' airplane—take-off and landing—was no longer than the wingspan of a Boeing 747 . . . you can begin to appreciate how far aviation has come in eighty years."[1] The 747 can now fly around the world in approximately forty-eight hours, a change made possible largely because of computer research. The computer, the most important invention in the history of man, has already altered life in the civilized world, but it promises to modify the future even more. Today's microcomputers could probably duplicate that feat in fewer than thirty years. In fact, in President Reagan's 1986 State of the Union address, he spoke of planes traveling at "Mach 25" by the 21st century—a trip around the world in two hours.

Life on this planet simply will not be the same in the 21st century. Most people are like passengers on a space shuttle through time. When they arrive in the 21st century, they will not be prepared for it. The Western world is on the verge of the greatest technological change known to man—and scarcely is a man alive whose life will be unaffected by it.

The National Aeronautics and Space Administration (NASA) sends astronauts into space only after rigorous training. Without this preparation they would not survive. Millions of our citizens will not be prepared for the future, or at least will not survive it very well, unless they prepare for it. The individual who does not plan for the future will be a victim of it.

This book will help you understand the revolutionary change in our times—which many call the "Information Age." We have already moved from the industrial age into the information age. This is rapidly transforming almost everything in life. Change is frightening and in some cases has undesirable effects on us—but today it is inevitable.

The future belongs to those who prepare for it vocationally, educationally, spiritually, and relationally. Whether you like it or not, you are in the race of your life—the race for the 21st century. This book will enable you, society, and the most important agencies of our nation to win that race.

The Race For The 21ST Century

STEP ONE

Understand the Future

___ 1 ___

Where Will Our Inventive Brains Take Us?

WHEN an organization paid $26,000 for an IBM System 06 Word Processor, I thought we had selected the "ultimate computer" for our needs. I had designed a temperament test with 183 variables that analyzed a person's temperament, strengths and abilities, vocational and local church aptitudes, and ten major weaknesses with suggestions of how to overcome them. In one minute a lone operator could run off a page while scoring and inputting the next test. The System 06 processed all the information and produced a beautiful, keepsake personalized letter from me to the person taking the test.

I was so thrilled with my new toy (as my wife called it) that I would stand in one spot, transfixed, watching it run. Within eight years and before we had processed 20,000 tests, the machine was *obsolete*. This week my wife's organization, Concerned Women for America (CWA), paid $27,000 for nine IBM PC's, several printers, long-distance input stations, and other pieces of equipment, including two high-speed laser printers that produce eight pages a minute and look much better than the pages from my beloved System 06.

In all probability these technological marvels will be obsolete in five years.

Where will the inventive brain of man take us? Frankly, I do not know, but everyone acknowledges a "high-tech" rate of change, which has so increased the amount of information available to us today that experts warn of the dangers of "an information glut" in this age called the "Information Age."

Truly, this is the age of the computer. Since the creation of Adam, nothing has altered the life of mankind like the computer. As a waist gunner on a B-29 in World War II, I operated a primitive computer that, when properly programmed with speed and distance, graphically increased our "kill" percentage over the old mounted fifty-caliber machine guns, which depended on human lead time to hit a moving target half a mile away. Since World War II, computers have invaded our lives and our homes, from the kitchen to the bedroom. DC-10's and 747's are flown by them; alarm clocks and traffic lights are controlled by them. They or their counterparts, microcomputer chips, operate cash registers, cameras, coffeepots, ovens, stereos, electric blankets, watches—the list is endless. Students learn by them, salesmen sell by them, big business forecasts by them, and joggers run by them.

In 1985 I visited the Future World Expo '85, which attracted over 85,000 visitors to the San Francisco Convention Center. I spent hours roaming around the huge display area, looking at futuristic gadgets of all kinds, including totally automatic cars that create electronic maps as one drives, a portable respirator that protects the wearer against allergies and air irritants, and jet shoes that allow the wearer to fly. But that's not all.

Overweight people will be pleased to learn about a collar that can be sewn into their clothes to absorb calories, allowing them to eat whatever they want without gaining weight. Singles can wear a wide belt, which serves as a compatability selector. When the right mate walks by, the belt sends off a mild shock wave to announce the good news. Hopefully the passerby isn't already married.

For those of us interested in emotional control, inventors are working on goggles that send a synchronized energy wave through earphones to create "euphoria, physical relaxation, and increased mental capabilities."[1]

Home computers have not proved as popular items as when they were first introduced, but they are not going away either. As their prices come down, they will become even more popular—particularly since they have been wedded to video games. It is a small jump for children from games to learning. In fact, because of their keen interest in video games, youngsters seem more comfortable with computers than do their parents. Many children spend hours daily at the computer keyboard.

Recently I watched my ten-year-old grandson reviewing his math tables and spelling on the family Apple II Computer. It is more like fun than work to him and his siblings. When I said, "Joel, if I get a portable computer so I can write while I ride on planes, will you teach me how to use it?" he grinned and replied, "Sure, Pop." His self-confidence certainly hasn't been diminished by his contact with computers.

As more practical programs are produced in color and accompanied by music and sound, they will become a staple part of family life—almost as necessary as the stove and refrigerator. Soon homemakers will keep track of recipes, finances, birthdays, addresses; you name the household task and the computer will do it. A friend in Dallas wants to put them in car radios so we can record our favorite songs or programs as we drive.

Recently "General Electric Co. (GE) introduced a system called a 'HomeMinder' that will wake its owners with toasted bagels, freshly brewed coffee and the 'Today' show. . . ." RCA predicts that the computerized TV set will be the center of the home's information and communications, including control of the telephone, word processor, banking, shopping, and anything we want it to do. It's only a step from this to computer-controlled security and lighting systems. This new combination of computer and TV should elevate the television sales industry beyond the $8.5 billion business of 1983.[2]

Making Friends with the Computer

When the first computers appeared in the fifties and early sixties, they seemed extraordinarily complex, and most people were afraid of them. Invented by electronic geniuses who talked in mathematical terms that confused us all, they required specially trained programmers and operators who formed their own "computer priesthood." We were mystified. At first, the cost was astronomical—from a quarter of a million dollars and up. Then along came computer chips and microchips.

Yesterday I saw a complete computer set, including printer, for less than $1,000—and the price continues to drop. Computers are becoming as common as typewriters. In our lifetime they have gone from a specialty item only governments could afford to a daily-use family item.

Computers have influenced our lives more than any of us realize, from the prescription drugs produced in computerized laboratories to computerized assembly lines. They have contributed to the destruction of the smokestack steel industry, which didn't have the foresight to see the computer coming. Still making payments on new smokestack style equipment, the industry can no longer compete with the prices charged by smaller computerized steel mills.

Many vocations are being automated out of existence by the computer-controlled robots on the assembly line—not just in the steel mills and auto plants but also in the textile mills and aerospace industry. If you don't become friends with the computer, you may be replaced by one at work. Secretaries will become an endangered species as soon as middle managers can input into $3,500 computers faster than secretaries can rough type and retype their letters. An estimated 5 percent of all high-level executives take computer training annually to avoid being left behind in their professions.

Computers have revolutionized everything from direct mail fund appeals to church record keeping, from testing students to averaging their grades at the end of the year. The computer print-out is as common as the daily paper. In fact, most papers are typeset by computers and printed on computer-controlled presses. *USA Today* is satellited daily to computerized receiver stations, where it is printed locally. So far the paperboy has not been replaced by a computer, but who knows how long before he, too, becomes obsolete?

Computerized Telecommunications

The potential for computerized telecommunications is incredible. I can "talk" into my office terminal in Washington, D.C.—even though the giant computer is two hours away by car—and get an answer back faster than I can type my question on the keyboard.

Lawyers can subscribe to a computerized legal service that gives them a print-out of comparable law cases within minutes, thus saving days of research. (And if you have hired an attorney lately, you know that one hour of computer time has to cost many times less than an hour of lawyer time.) The medical profession has not, of course, been outdone. Doctors can pump examination details, vital statistics, and sickness symptoms into a computer to receive expert diagnostic and remedial suggestions from the best minds in the medical profession. Ministers can subscribe to computerized sermon and illustration helps to supplement their research. Almost no profession has gone untouched by the computer.

The Computer and Outer Space

The National Aeronautics and Space Administration's (NASA) incredible space-age achievements would never have been possible without the computer. Now we are building space stations and have an operational space shuttle that has already converted space exploration to commercial use. Many research experiments and manufacturing techniques can be done faster and cheaper in the weightlessness of space. One NASA administrator has predicted that by the 21st century space-age commercialization "could generate $500 billion worldwide."[3] No longer do science fiction writers alone talk about people living in outer space. With the computer, man's inhabiting the moon and other planets is conceivable.

President Ronald Reagan was ridiculed by the press for suggesting during his 1984 campaign that the "Star Wars" defense, now known as Strategic Defense Initiative (SDI), was worth researching as a nonnuclear deterrent to the Soviet Union's ultimate desire to conquer the United States. I knew it was valid because I had heard retired Major General Daniel Graham lecture on what he called "The High Frontier"—or using existing space equipment to defend against unfriendly rockets. Now, of course, even the press realizes the validity of the president's space defense system because the Russians registered such alarm at our plans to initiate the system. They may not be able to build very good computer systems, but they certainly understand them and recognize their potential. Computers make SDI possible.

Within five years (if we can stop traitors from selling our secrets to the Russians), we can leap so far ahead of the Russians in our military capabilities in space that they will no longer be a threat to the United States. Robert Cooper, director of the Defense Advanced Research Projects Agency (DARPA), informed the House Armed Services Committee that we will fulfill the air force's long-standing dream of having a "transatmospheric vehicle," which will be capable of taking off, orbiting the entire earth, destroying its target, and returning to base within an hour and twenty minutes by the mid-1990s. "'It could be used for global reconnaissance to get to any point on the earth in perhaps half an hour,'" Cooper said.[4] Can you imagine flying such a plane without computers? Impossible!

I fly a twin-engine plane that has a cruise speed of 230 MPH. Once when I picked up a 100-knot tail wind and was descending slightly, my digital ground speed indicator showed I was traveling at 358 MPH. I couldn't believe how fast things happened in the cockpit! I had to slow the plane down just to keep up with my navigation aids. Can you imagine manually flying a hundred times that fast? Without a computer it would be impossible.

If the computers of our world were suddenly to go dead, life as we know it would come to a screeching halt. Planes would not fly; trains would not run; banks and retail and grocery stores would be forced to close; and even the government would be shut down. We are a computer-dependent society. And plans are underway to make us even more so.

You have doubtless heard of the "cashless society" in which money will become obsolete and everyone will use his computer code mark and number. I asked my banker recently when a cashless society would become feasible. He replied, "As soon as we can devise a way to keep computer thieves out of the system." Human greed and dishonesty have slowed "cashless society" plans because so many clever ways have been found to defraud the system that it is still not safe. But be sure of this, it will come. This not only prefigures the totalitarian society that Orwell envisioned for 1984 but frighteningly foreshadows the society of the anti-Christ prophesied in the Bible.

Of course, if all the computers in the Western world stopped for a single day, our nation would be plunged into hopeless chaos, and we would be extremely vulnerable to a Soviet takeover. Talk about "the ultimate weapon"—a computer scrambler could be it!

Computerized Television Sets

If, as some suggest, the computer is the most influential invention of the past thirty years, television certainly cannot be far behind. Word from the TV industry indicates that the sets of the future are going high-tech or computerized. Unbelievable detail will be possible on the screen, and with the touch of a button, a picture can be frozen in place. Another button will activate the printer, supplying a color print-out of any picture one chooses. Still another button will create a separate image in the corner of the set so one can watch two channels simultaneously! Some people already wear out the dials on their television sets as they switch back and forth from one football game to another. Soon people will be able to view two football games or two soap operas at the same time. That may sharply improve the Nielsen ratings (but not do much for marriages).

The future, whether Orwellian, prophetic, or just the 21st century, is coming in like a flood. You need to know what it contains in order to cope with it. The next two chapters will examine the forecasts of the most popular futurist thinkers of our day. You may not agree with some of their conclusions because of philosophical differences, but their scientific research of today's trends has provided them a valid base to foresee what life will be like in the nineties and the 21st century. You will find their observations interesting—and in many cases valuable.

2

Will We Break Under the Pressure of Change?

A study of the future would not be complete without an examination of the theories of Alvin Toffler, one of the foremost futuristic writers of our time. His book, *Future Shock,* hit the public like a bombshell in 1971 and has sold close to 6 million copies. His 1980 sequel, *The Third Wave,* sold over 500,000 copies in its $14.95 hardback edition.

Such literary success has opened incredible opportunities for him to influence the leading centers of academia. Many companies hire him as a consultant to help them prepare for the inevitable changes ahead, causing them to redirect and retrain their entire staffs before the firms become obsolete. In the past, he has been able to steer profitable firms into entirely new fields before profits fell, allowing them to take advantage of the advances in high-tech inventions. The industrial giants who have fallen on hard times or entered bankruptcy because they resisted the changes brought on by progress—or did not see them coming—could have saved themselves considerable grief had they consulted him or his theories about the future of their industries.

Although his liberal philosophical base, the apparent absence of interest in religious values, and his lack of understanding of the conservative mood swing in the Western world make his conclusions in these areas suspect, no serious student of the future can approach the subject without a basic understanding of his two principal works. They are so important that a brief review of each is in order here.

Future Shock

Change has so accelerated in the Western world during the past few years, Toffler says, that millions of individuals cannot cope with it. Consequently they are developing a serious illness which he calls "future shock." Change has left many the unwilling victims of "progress," and they are unprepared to face life in the present, much less in the future. Who can deny that during the decade and a half since he first diagnosed the problem, there has been an alarming increase in suicide, drug and alcohol addiction, divorce, crime, and many other signs that millions of our numbers are less content with the quality of their lives?

Toffler predicts, "Unless man quickly learns to control the rate of change in his personal affairs as well as in society at large, we are doomed to a massive adaptational breakdown."[1] Of course, Toffler makes no allowance for divine resources, which can help a person cope with all of life's circumstances, even the unknown.

Toffler's antidote for future shock is to understand the trends of the last three decades in order to project them into the future and then prepare for that future. He stresses that noting the direction of accelerated change helps to reveal the unknown mysteries that will realistically come upon us. Knowledge reduces the changes to life-size and enables us to prepare for them. Four of the important trends he mentions are transience, the super-industrial revolution, a new educational philosophy, and a computer-controlled society.

1. Transience

According to Toffler, things, people, places, organizations, and ideas are the basic components of all situations.[2] A person's relationship to these elements will structure his situation in life and paint his view of the future. Despite Toffler's omission of faith, he is certainly correct in observing that increasing change in these five areas can unsettle even the most secure soul, fomenting bewilderment, disorientation, and frustration—thus making society so transient that it becomes unstable. For instance, industry has been moving from the cold climates of the north to the fifteen warmer states of the "sun belt," where corporation taxes and less unionism attract manufacturers. This has relocated more millions of people than the divorce rate, and consequently even school-age children seldom finish the year without the loss of friends. Long-term solid relationships with people are the exception today rather than the rule, even in our churches or neighborhoods, clubs and organizations. The class reunion will probably not be popular in the 21st century because close and meaningful relationships will hardly have time to develop.

2. The Super-Industrial Revolution

The industrial revolution replaced the centuries-old rural society with what we have called modern society. Over the last thirty to forty years the West has been accelerating toward what Toffler calls "The Super-Industrial Society." Toffler warns us,

> We are creating a new society. Not a changed society. Not an extended, larger-than-life version of our present society. But a new society. . . .
> Only by accepting the premise that we are racing toward a wholly new stage of eco-technological development—the new super-industrial stage—can we make sense of our era . . . [and] free our imaginations to grapple with the future.[3]

Toffler also suggests that the future will produce an "aqua culture," a society that learns to harness and develop the sea, particularly what lies at the bottom of the sea. After all, three-fourths of the earth's surface is under water. We are now drilling oil at sea and providing vast amounts of seafood from the ocean, but that is just a beginning. There are yet to be discovered untold riches in minerals, ore, and diamonds. High-tech inventions will provide for their exploitation, employing millions of laborers in new jobs.

In view of this prospect, Who owns the sea? becomes a monumental question. Does ownership extend 200 miles offshore of each adjacent nation? The Communist-dominated United Nations' "Treaty of the Sea," proposed under the Carter administration, almost gave away America's seafaring birthright. Designed by those in the UN who advocate "one world" (the molding of all the countries of the world into one society), it would have permitted the high-tech countries of the West to develop these resources—and then share most of the profits with the Third World (the "undeveloped" countries of the world). Does that sound like Karl Marx's plan of taking from the haves and giving to the have nots? Fortunately, the state of Texas elected to Congress a Christian named Jack Fields who blew the whistle on that plot early in the Reagan administration. This treaty has been temporarily buried in the sea of UN and congressional bureaucracy where it will remain unless a liberal president revives it.

But regardless of who controls the sea, high technology will soon make the aqua-culture commonplace in our society, offering incredible new opportunities to entrepreneurs, investors, and the venturesome.

3. A New Educational Philosophy

Just as Toffler sees the "craggy outlines of the new society emerging from the mists of tomorrow," he sees "evidence that one of our most critical sub-systems—education—is dangerously malfunctioning."

Toffler's morbid analysis of the U.S. educational system was truly prophetic in 1971, when his book came out. Now many people are realizing the accuracy of his predictions.

> What passes for education today, even in our "best" schools and colleges, is a hopeless anachronism. . . .
> . . . our schools face backward toward a dying system, rather than forward to the emerging new society. Their vast energies are applied to cranking out Industrial Men—people tooled for survival in a system that will be dead before they are. . . .
> . . . we must create a super-industrial education system. And to do

this, we must search for our objectives and methods in the future, rather than the past.[4]

Toffler suggests that education must begin by generating

successive, alternative images of the future—assumptions about the kinds of jobs, professions, and vocations that may be needed twenty to fifty years in the future; assumptions about the kind of family forms and human relationships that will prevail; the kinds of ethical and moral problems that will arise; the kind of technology that will surround us and the organizational structures with which we must mesh.[5]

Then, Toffler says, "we can deduce the nature of the cognitive and affective skills that the people of tomorrow will need to survive the accelerative thrust."[6]

Having been a careful observer in our humanistically dominated public schools, I do not share Mr. Toffler's hope that the public educational institutions have the capacity to prepare our present generation for the 21st century. If they can't teach Johnny to read and write adequately, how can they establish a foundation for the high-tech computer age?

Until we get serious about teaching Johnny to be a good reader, we will not solve the functional illiteracy of the present age—much less the one to come. I believe that an advanced reading ability will remain the foundation for all learning and that students educated at home or in Christian or other private schools have a distinct advantage because such schools major in teaching the basics.

If public education is the vehicle for ushering in a generation of information-age thinkers, we are indeed in for a national future shock.

4. A Computer-controlled Society

There is always the possibility that voice-activated computers will come to Johnny's rescue, provided they can be made to analyze results and read them for him. In fact, a step in this direction has already been taken. OLIVER (an acronym for On-Line Interactive Vicarious Expediter and Responder) is now under consideration and will probably make its appearance soon.

Toffler describes OLIVER in his book:

> It could store information about his friends' preferences . . . . data about traffic routes, the weather, stock prices, etc. The device could be set to remind him of his wife's birthday—or to order flowers automatically. It could renew his magazine subscriptions, pay the rent on time, order razor blades and the like. . . .
> . . . moreover, it would tap into a worldwide pool of data stored in libraries, corporate files, hospitals, retail stores, banks, government agencies and universities.[7]

OLIVER's children and grandchildren may be capable of much more than the functions of a secretary and research assistant. Someday the computer could become the owner's other half or representative. It is theoretically possible to construct an OLIVER that would analyze the content of its owner's words, scrutinize his choices, deduce his value system, update its own program to reflect changes in his values, and ultimately handle larger and larger decisions for him.

Thus OLIVER would know how its owner would, in all likelihood, react to various suggestions made at a committee meeting. (Meetings could take place among groups of OLIVERs representing their respective owners, without the owners themselves being present. Indeed, some "computer-mediated" conferences of this type have already been held by the experimenters.)[8]

Adapting to Future Shock

In so few pages it is impossible to do justice to Toffler's book which, like Pandora's box, opened a whole new world that is fifteen years closer than when he first penned it. Read this book for yourself—if not to agree with his conclusions, at least to evaluate the inventions, policies, and trends that will become reality in the not-so-distant future.

We need to be aware of coming change in order to utilize our natural adaptive energies to cope with that change. But as we shall see, we will have to train ourselves or pick up additional education to enable us to maintain some degree of control over our future. The more control we exercise over our circumstances, the less of what I call "pressure" we experience—or, in the words of Toffler, the less impact future shock will have on us.

The Third Wave

Toffler's second major futuristic work hit the bookstands one decade later. Although it did not register the same bombshell impact, it has been accorded wide acclaim. Actually, I liked it better than *Future Shock*, for it seemed to convey a more mature presentation of the concepts that were burning in his heart.

Essentially, he sees "colliding waves of change" making life uncertain for everyone, even though different people live in different waves, depending on the advancement of their culture. A good way to grasp his concept is as follows:

First Wave: Agricultural man—Adam to the seventeenth century.

Second Wave: Industrial revolution—seventeenth century to mid-twentieth century.

Third Wave: Technocratic (high-tech) age—since around 1955.

For six thousand years man lived in an agricultural society (Toffler suggests about eight thousand years before Christ). Then along came the Industrial Revolution around 1650–1750 (the same time that the Pilgrims, Puritans, and other early settlers were migrating to America). This was the dawn of the Second Wave, the inventive period that brought on electricity, steam power, and eventually gasoline-powered engines. Industry, retailers, and a variety of services at first started out simply but gradually grew into enormous corporations. In ". . . 1800 there were only 335 corporations in the United States, most of them devoted to such quasi-public activities as building canals or running turnpikes. . . . By 1901 the world's first billion-dollar corporation—United States Steel—appeared on the scene, a concentration of assets unimaginable in any earlier period."[9]

After that came automobiles—the first auto assembly plant in 1913 with the Model T Ford. It was followed by corporate behemoths such as General Motors, Ford Motor Company, General Electric, IBM, AT&T, Xerox, and others whose legions of employees and gross incomes were larger than the standing armies and annual taxable incomes of many countries throughout the world.

The nuclear family (the traditional family without extended relatives), the factory-style school, and the corporation were the definitive social institutions of all Second Wave societies. Toffler describes the life-style of this wave: "Most people followed a standard life trajectory: reared in a nuclear family, they moved en masse through factorylike schools, then entered the service of a large corporation, private or public. A key Second Wave institution dominated each phase of the life-style."[10]

What Toffler labeled "the Super-Industrial Revolution" in *Future Shock,* he now identifies as the Third Wave, the information age.

To understand Toffler's waves and our relationship to the Third Wave in particular, we must keep in mind that waves of the sea are not always separate and distinct; sometimes they converge, causing turmoil before the stronger wave takes distinct shape. Such is the case with the Third Wave. The most highly developed Second Wave societies are the ones that started to enter the Third Wave first (the United States, Japan, Canada, some western European countries, and such high-tech Asian countries as Korea, Singapore, and Hong Kong).

During the transition period or the indistinct phase, both waves can be found at the same time. We still have such corporate dinosaurs as U.S. Steel, but they are dying painfully before our eyes as newer, leaner steel-producing plants appear that are capable of being more competitive with foreign imports. The Third Wave, according to Toffler, began in the mid-fifties, really started to gather momentum in the sixties, and should be in full swing by the turn of the century (except in many Third World countries where education and development are so primitive that citizens are still living in the First Wave, or agricultural age).

Since the mid-fifties nuclear power has begun to replace fossil fuel as the primary source of energy in some industries. The computer invaded all areas of technology, so much that we now talk in terms of high tech. All of this has generated a vocational change and standard of living that is moving us from the Second to the Third Wave.

Decentralization

In essence, Toffler's book traces our advancement from the industrial age to the information age. The number of blue-collar workers is decreasing; the number of office workers, planners, computer programmers, engineers, technicians, and service personnel is sharply increasing. At the core of it all is the decentralization of management. The company president used to be lord of the corporation; the school superintendent ran the district; the bank president managed the bank through regional vice presidents. This kind of leadership, Toffler claims, must yield control to middle managers because of the sheer weight of the information glut and the inability of one human being to stay on top of everything. No longer does the chief executive officer of a large corporation control the business; rather, chosen leaders exercise dominion through the managers they appoint.

Toffler illustrates his concept in the bureaucracy of government, reflecting the truism so often uttered by conservatives, "The more things change, the more they remain the same." After fifty years of liberal administrators who have practiced the philosophy of "spend-spend-spend," bringing us almost to a trillion dollars of national debt, in 1980 we elected a conservative president who ran on a platform of "cut the size of government spending and reduce taxes." Within six years the trillion-dollar debt increased to two trillion dollars, despite the promises of this president.

Actually, presidents have less power than most people think. If a president appoints a secretary of state that the bureaucrats in the State Department disapprove, they can either keep the secretary from being confirmed by the Senate or make it impossible for him to impose his or the president's will on foreign policy. One must subsequently ask, Who elected the bureaucrats in the State Department? Is a federal government with almost three million employees out of control? Or is it impossible for one person to control government?

Stockholders are asking the same questions of corporate presidents. We have spawned a generation of self-centered individuals who don't care who pays their salary; they will "do their own thing." Toffler ignores, and most students of futurism fail to understand, the biblical principle that two cannot "walk together, unless they be agreed" (Amos 3:3). The most important principle in personnel selection—whether it's hiring a baby sitter or an executive secretary for the president of General Motors—is philosophy of life.

If I am a Christian conservative committed to raising my child with traditional values, should I hire a secular humanist baby sitter, perhaps a homosexual, who has decided that a five-year-old should early be taught to "practice his sexuality"? The answer is obvious. Many unwitting parents have compromised their children by providing competent care, only to discover that the baby sitter had more liberated ideas on sexuality than they did. Two can't walk together except they are agreed—at least not in happy harmony.

Corporate presidents make the same mistake when they equate competence with skills and personality. A secretary may type 180 words a minute, transcribe every word flawlessly, and keep the boss on schedule without a hitch. But if committed to a different ideology, the secretary will hinder the boss' accomplishments whenever the opportunity to do so arises. Try, for example, to get in to see a conservative president (of the country or a corporation) who is flanked by liberal staff members. Your phone calls are rarely received, you can hardly get an appointment, and you will wait in line while those who share the appointment secretary's ideology have ready access.

This type of run-around is all too familiar to me. Yet when confronted with our message or cause, many presidents have asked, "Why haven't I heard about this before?" The answer sits in the next room—a "competent" secretary. True competence cannot omit ideology or philosophy of life. Of one thing I am confident: as high-tech computers and accessories enable the office paper mill to turn out more documents, copies, and memos than any one person can assimilate, loyalty and philosophical agreement will rank increasingly high on the priority scale for selecting competent leaders of the future. And the more important the position, the higher ranking that priority will take.

The Point of It All

As decentralization of authority comes down to an increasingly well-educated population, they will demand a more significant role in the decision-making process, Toffler says. He predicts an ever-increasing involvement of citizens in the process of government. We have already been observing a more insistent grassroots political pattern, from Proposition 13 tax initiative actions to sidewalk demonstrations, from pro-life to anti-life and gay life. M.A.D.D.

(Mothers Against Drunk Driving) has been very effective in activating government against the principal cause of over 50 percent of our traffic fatalities. My wife's organization, Concerned Women for America (C.W.A.), and other groups have launched a campaign to get alcohol commercials taken off television. The National Federation for Decency has launched a drive to rid America of pornography—and the trend goes on, from nuclear freeze demonstrations to ordinary citizens running for public office. In the Second Wave, "leadership" was executed by a tightly knit group. The Third Wave will reduce it in the minds of people so that almost everyone can aspire for some role in the decision-making process—community, city, state, and national. If Christians wake up and view this as a golden opportunity to take a more active role in politics, media, and education—to become "the salt of the earth" (Matt. 5:13)—we can have a much greater influence on the 21st century than we have had on the twentieth.

The Electronic Cottage

One projection Toffler makes for his Third Wave society should have great interest to all Christians and lovers of the family. Toffler says:

> We are about to revolutionize our homes as well. . . .
> . . . the new production system could shift literally millions of jobs out of the factories and offices into which the Second Wave swept them and right back where they came from originally: the home. If this were to happen, every institution we know, from the family to the school and the corporation, would be transformed.[11]

If you have spent an hour each day driving or commuting to work—as millions of people do—working at home can become very appealing. When one thinks about it, nine hours spent at work, added to driving time and seven hours for sleep, means that the average person is afforded no more than five hours a night for family, church, friends, and activities. Turning one's home into a cottage industry would change all that as many workers are discovering.

This idea is not as revolutionary as it sounds. Toffler reminds us that an unmeasured but appreciable amount of work is already being done at home by such people as salesmen and saleswomen who work by phone or visit, and only occasionally touch base at the office; by architects and designers; by a burgeoning pool of specialized consultants in many industries; . . . and by many other categories of white-collar, technical, and professional people.

These are, moreover, among the most rapidly expanding work classifications, and when we suddenly make available technologies that can place a low-cost "work station" in any home, providing it with a "smart" typewriter, perhaps, along with a facsimile machine or computer console and teleconferencing equipment, the possibilities for home work are radically extended.[12]

A Western Electric official claimed that "600 to 700 of [his] 2,000 [employees] could . . . work at home." The manufacturing manager of Hewlett-Packard admitted that technologically 250 of his 1,000 employees "could work at home." A Canadian vice president stated that "fully 75 percent" of his 300 employees "could work at home if we provided the necessary communications technology."[13]

A Christian attorney recently explained to me why he converted his garage into a law office so he could work at home. "I like being there every night when the children come home from school. We will only spend these few years together, so I want to make the most of them. There will be plenty of time for the big office in the city later—if I want it. Now I'm majoring in being a father!"

Given the high cost of office space, air conditioning, heating, lighting, clothing, transportation, and meals, industry and its employees may find it more cost-effective to remain at home. It will, of course, take a self-disciplined, organized individual and some system of accountability. But for time saving, lack of interruptions (in Christian organizations "fellowship" during work hours can be a terrible time drain), better work environment, and family unity, "the electronic cottage"—or, as some futurists call it, "the cottage industry"—has much to commend it. In fact, it is my favorite Third Wave idea. I now have two full-time employees and one part-time employee who work at home.

A Final Word

Although I recommend that you read Toffler's _The Third Wave,_ I do not agree with all his suggestions or conclusions because some of them conflict with my Christian perspective. I reject the theory that values are situational. To me values do not change, since they come from God's Word in the Bible.

Most futurists misunderstand the nature of man and moral absolutes. They seem to believe that man is getting better and better—the old "perfectability of man" theory of Jean Jacques Rousseau. They don't realize that man fell in the Garden of Eden and that God has given him moral absolutes by which to live (thou shalt not steal, kill, lie, commit adultery). If those absolutes are not established as a minimum standard for society, it will descend into the maelstrom of civil chaos, which typically leads to totalitarianism.

Toffler seems to suggest that we should be open to change, but I think we need to remember that all change does not lead to improvement. John Dewey, a man Toffler admires, was addicted to change for its own sake (educators call it "the evolution of change"). We all know what Dewey's "progressive" modifications have done to our once-great school system.

I am more apt to believe the truth of the old adage, "If something isn't broke, don't fix it." I am not saying that we must resist all technological change. I believe that we should be open to innovative thinking so long as we can be reasonably assured that it will lead to real progress.

I am afraid that if the Third Wave is not guided by persons committed to a moral standard of behavior and a Constitution that guarantees an orderly process of government, this wave could result in a hurricane of anarchy followed by the imperialism of the strongest government in the history of mankind. We who live in the twilight of the twentieth century have a destiny to create, as Toffler says, but we had better base it on tried and proven principles of the past rather than blind change in the future. Otherwise, we will bequeath chains instead of freedom to our children. I am convinced that the best procedure to assure an improved 21st century is for Christians to get involved in the process of change and guide it according to biblical principles. That is why God gave us the Bible in the first place.

3

Will Knowledge Be Power in the 21st Century?

*I*N October of 1982 John Naisbitt's book, *Megatrends,* became an instant best seller. Called "a road map to the 21st century" and a "field guide of the future," it has become the most talked-about book in the eighties. Every serious student of the future and those interested in the quality of life in the 21st century should read it. He has effectively built on the work of other futurists before him and has added his careful analysis of the trends of the past few years, providing us with an examination of the ten trends that he believes are molding the future.

John Naisbitt is best known as a social forecaster. An author and a consultant to such corporations as IBM, General Electric, AT&T, and many others, he regularly publishes the "John Naisbitt Trend Letter," read regularly by progressive businessmen. His research is based on the science of newspaper content analysis, a method developed by the U.S. intelligence community during World War II to determine what was really going on in Germany. The Naisbitt group claims to continually monitor six thousand local newspapers each month. By statistically analyzing them, the group can establish trends (assuming that papers really do print "all the news that's fit to print"). As we shall see, they consistently omit the Christian news as though we are not significant enough to warrant space, and their liberal bias makes them often less than fair in reporting conservative activities. Otherwise, their analysis of trends is quite valuable.

Naisbitt lists eleven megatrends (those already covered by Toffler will be skimmed):

Megatrend I: From an Industrial Society to an Information Society

You are already familiar with this phenomenon, which Toffler describes as the Second Wave and the Third Wave. In 1956 white-collar workers started to outnumber blue-collar workers for the first time. In 1957 the Russians launched Sputnik and the space age, which is dependent on the computer. In the next twenty-five years, information jobs (those dependent upon technical knowledge) went from only 17 percent of our nation's positions to 65 percent.[1]

At the turn of the century farmers made up one-third of the work force. In 1979 clerks became the largest profession; then came professional workers identified as ". . . lawyers, teachers, engineers, computer programmers, systems analysts, doctors, architects, accountants, librarians, newspaper reporters, social workers, nurses, and clergy."[2] There were 7.5 million professional people in 1960; that number more than doubled in twenty-one years to 16.4 million, totaling "almost 17 percent of the work force (and almost half of those are women)."[3] By 1982 farmers were only 3 percent of the work force!

Very little capital is required to start a business today, in contrast to one hundred years ago. Back then an innovative idea could die because very few had the resources to capitalize on it. (My mother's family likes to tell the story that my grandfather, a Detroit teamster, had an inventor friend who offered to sell him "one-tenth of his new company for $2,500." Unfortunately, my grandfather didn't have the money. His friend was Henry Ford!)

Note the trend! In 1950, 93,000 new businesses were started per year. "Today [1982], we are creating new companies in this country at the rate of more than 600,000 a year."[4] Naisbitt's classic conclusion is that "the new source of power is not money in the hands of a few but information in the hands of many."[5] Knowledge has become the primary business, and the transformation from the industrial society to the informational society is proceeding at an accelerating pace. He points out that the younger giant corporations are mostly information companies—AT&T, IBM, ITT, XEROX, RCA.[6]

Like Toffler, Naisbitt ties the computer to the electrifying increases of information-related jobs in the future and challenges his readers to make friends with the computer as soon as possible.

Megatrend II: From Forced Technology to High Tech, High Touch

To illustrate what he is saying, Naisbitt uses the advent of television, which is high-tech impersonal. Shortly after it was introduced, there was an explosion of "the group therapy movement, which led to the personal growth movement, which in turn led to the human potential movement and Erhard Seminar Training (est), transcendental meditation (TM), Yoga, Zen, and so forth—all very high touch" to compensate for it.[7] Because man needs the touch of other people, whenever his life is invaded by high tech (in which he interacts with machines more than people), he subconsciously reaches out for high touch. (Churches should be very conscious of this, undergirding the need for people to be with other people.)

Computers and other high-tech inventions are here to stay, and the future will be filled with some we can scarcely dream of today. But somehow they will have to make peace with the human element in the operators—the need for companionship. Naisbitt suggests an increasing return to outdoor activities.

I have observed an incredible increase in the number of participation sports. For instance the high-school track on which I jog each morning is next to a softball diamond which for years stood empty most of the time. Not any more! Every Saturday some group appears for a game, from eight o'clock on—not little leaguers, but their fathers! Could that be an involuntary reaction to high tech?

Megatrend III: From a National Economy
to a World Economy

Like most futurist thinkers, including Toffler, Naisbitt is a globist (a person who promotes such strong economic and social interrelations between nations that the world becomes one united community). This may be influenced by the well-publicized activities of the trilateral commission that meets annually to discuss interdependent economic subjects or by the fact that the speed of travel has brought nations much closer together.

The once-great U.S. industrial complex that made us the world's leading industrial nation is no more, Naisbitt reminds us. From 1973 (the year of the oil crisis) to 1981, our "productivity growth decreased to about 0.4 percent per year. And in 1979, productivity growth declined 2 percent."[8] He then notes that Japan is taking our place and is being challenged by Singapore, South Korea, and Brazil. (But don't worry: we're no longer an industrial society anyhow.) Even though we still have the world's highest gross national product (GNP), we no longer enjoy the highest standard of living. According to Naisbitt, "Sweden, Denmark, West Germany, Switzerland, Holland and Norway" have surpassed us.[9]

The best way for America to face the future, Naisbitt explains, is to put aside the industrial society and concentrate full speed on the information economy. But it is difficult for most people to envision an increase in the GNP without the development of products.

Two factors have "played the key role in transforming the planet into a global economic village: the jet airplane and the communication satellite."[10] We can traverse the ocean in less than five hours and also talk to other continents instantly by satellite. The time delay (which he calls "information float") that kept people of different nations days apart throughout the centuries is being reduced sharply by telecommunications. "The information float collapsed because of a telecommunications infrastructure that grows more sophisticated, and more accessible, every day. By the end of this decade, for instance, this world will have one billion telephones, all interconnected and almost all capable of dialing direct to any other."[11]

Because of cheap labor, Third World countries will become the

manufacturing countries of the future. Since the world auto industry is getting saturated, he predicts the death of many auto companies and, as we have seen in recent days, the emergence of the
auto industry on an international scale. He observes that Renault,
which owns part of American Motors, is buying into Volvo, that
"GM owns 34 percent of Japan's Isuzu," that Chrysler is a partner of
Peugeot, that Nissan, "which owns 37 percent of Spain's Motor
Iberica, has a joint venture with Alfa Romeo," and that GM and
Toyota are partners in California.[12]

Once the world's nations are economically dependent on one another, "peace" may become more appealing, Naisbitt predicts. Even
border hostilities could throw off a nation's entire economy, plung-
ing it into unemployment and depression. What an opportunity for
a super-dictator to threaten interdependent nations into submission!
Just as many unthinking Americans in the sixties voiced a "Better
red than dead" philosophy, the 21st-century interdependent citizen
may announce, "Better less freedom than unemployment." Naisbitt
says that we are already "so economically intertwined with Japan
that if we have any problems with Japan today, we are going to
work them out . . . the same will be true globally."[13]

Megatrend IV: From Short Term to Long Term

No one can accuse John Naisbitt of timidity. He pointedly ac-
cuses American business managers of being "the cause of our national economic decline. We hear a lot of alibis, but their
preoccupation with short-term results and quantitative measure-
ments of performance were responsible for the neglect of the kinds
of investments and innovations necessary to increase the nation's
capacity to create wealth." He also indicts America's business
schools, insisting that they "must accept a large share of the responsibility for the short-term numbers orientation of American business. For years they have been turning out MBAs who, because of
their training, fancy they could manage anything because they
know the numbers."[14]

Naisbitt quotes Michael P. Schulhof, vice president and director
of the Sony Corporation of America, who said: "'The short-term

and frequently shortsighted positions win out with disturbing regularity because American business is top-heavy with the ever-expanding numbers of business school graduates who are trained advocates of the short-term profit.

"'It is not entirely coincidence,' Schulhof says, 'that the same years that have seen industry increasingly, almost exclusively, run by financially oriented business school graduates have also seen the worst productivity performance since the Depression.'"[15]

Fortunately, Naisbitt can point to signs that some leaders and boards of directors are beginning to see the need for long-term plans. Every company that endures will have to plan for change, study the market, and inaugurate new product lines before their present products become obsolete. He quotes General Electric, one of the more long-range thinking corporations, as explaining that it is "'in the business of creating businesses'"—not merely light bulbs and electricity.[16]

Megatrend V: From Centralization to Decentralization

"We must get government off the back of the people" served as the theme of candidate Ronald Reagan's speeches in 1964. The Naisbitt research team sees it as the wave of the future and an organizational necessity. We have grown up with our eyes riveted upon Washington, D.C.—and with very little interest in local or state government. In actuality, our community and state governments have more control over our lives than the federal government. For example, "during the 1970s . . . Congress enacted 3,359 laws, but the state of New York passed 9,780. All fifty state legislatures passed some 250,000 laws in the 1970s. Those figures confirm that the burden of regulation has shifted to the states, a trend that was powerfully underscored with the advent of the Reagan presidency."[17]

Naisbitt, like Toffler, believes that power from the top down stultifies, whereas power flowing from the bottom up invigorates:

The failure of centralized, top-down solutions has been accompanied by a huge upsurge in grassroots political activity everywhere in the

United States. Some twenty million Americans are now organized around issues of local concern. About 25 percent of the population of any neighborhood in the country say they are members of a neighborhood group. Neighborhood groups are becoming powerful and demanding greater participation in decision making.

Because of a long tradition of local control, education is a natural issue for community activism. . . . Advocates of public education walk a tightrope between the demand for local control and the need for additional funding. Inflation and tax reform have made locally funded education a thing of the past. Consequently, state funding of local education has increased greatly during the past decade. But educators and parents have learned, to their dismay, that outside funds can also mean outside control. Many local education groups have now rallied around the sentiment "State (or federal) aid without state control."[18]

This, of course, as suggested in the previous chapter, offers Christians an ideal opportunity to be "the salt" of their community by running for and getting elected to their school boards, city councils, or other elective bodies. We need to take a more active part in community affairs; otherwise people who do not share our moral concerns will fill the vacuum we leave.

Megatrend VI: From Institutional Help to Self-Help

In the early days of America, everyone had to carry his own load. Then as liberal-socialist teachers invaded the schoolhouse and the welfare state mentality set in, we raised several generations that assumed our institutions—government, schools, corporations, and so on—would take care of us. The inability of government to care for us from the cradle to the grave began to become apparent in the late 1960s. The 1970s launched a self-help movement that involved "community groups acting to prevent crime," community projects aiding the elderly and handicapped, and medical plans offering instruction programs from improved eating habits and vitamins to physical exercise.[19]

Previous generations had no problem keeping fit; they worked so hard each day just to stay alive that fitness programs weren't necessary. But the 1950s and 1960s produced so many overfed, under-worked, flabby citizens that we became a nation of health hazards. When a president's commission on health urged all Americans to get regular exercise—either jogging or taking long walks—I remember laughing to myself, That idea will never catch on. I think about that comment each time I jog on the Washington Mall near my office—and I almost get run over by other joggers!

The Prestonwood Baptist Church in Dallas invited Dr. Ken Cooper of aerobics fame (a member of the Bible class I teach at Prestonwood every Sunday) to sponsor a jog one Sunday afternoon, terminating in the auditorium, where he gave his testimony. Two thousand showed up for the first jog! We are becoming a nation of health nuts—living longer though not always better.

Space does not permit mention of Naisbitt's other excellent illustrations on self-help—from birth alternatives to home schooling to home gardening (according to Gallup, 33 million grow some of their own food).

Megatrend VII: The Entrepreneurial Explosion

One phenomenon we cannot afford to overlook is the accelerating growth in entrepreneurs. We have already noted that in 1983 over 600,000 new jobs were created and self-employment was booming. In this country a person with a good idea, the courage to take a chance, and the determination to work diligently can realize the American dream. Even corporate executives who take the plunge into self-employment report that they prefer the independence, experience greater job satisfaction, and in some cases achieve greater financial success. As we have seen, with the continuing rise of the information society and the lower prices of computers, one doesn't have to be rich to become an entrepreneur. Millions more of us will try it before the 21st century. Work is a necessary part of life; since we have to work, we might as well do it for ourselves.

Some Christians have difficulty with this idea. When they read "But seek first the kingdom of God and His righteousness, and all these things shall be added to you" (Matt. 6:33) or "Set your mind on things above, not on things on the earth" (Col. 3:2), they falsely conclude that working regular hours for someone else is a better fulfillment of those verses than working for oneself. The key lies in maintaining a right attitude toward God, no matter where or how we work. Admittedly, success in your own business is often dependent on sixteen-hour days, six days a week—at first. Later, however, a thriving business will usually provide the owner with more flexibility of schedule, greater financial resources, and increased influence. The secret to simultaneous spiritual and entrepreneurial success is to keep our eyes on the ultimate goal of serving God and to continue to rank personal fellowship with Him as our number one priority.

Megatrend VIII: From Representative Democracy to Participatory Democracy

During a 1970s "sit-in" in the president's offices of the University of California at San Diego, I heard long-haired, barefoot hippies demanding "the right to be a part of the decision-making process." That "right" has become a national quest, which Naisbitt believes is propelling us farther and farther from the days when citizens were content to elect officials and leave the governing to them. Now 231 million people seem to be clamoring for a piece of the decision-making process. He believes that "people whose lives are affected by a decision must be part of the process of arriving at that decision."[20]

As I write these words, I am reminded of the historic Southern Baptist Convention that I recently attended. Over 45,000 people registered, and during the business sessions it seemed that all of them wanted to speak. We heard an unbelievable number of resolutions—far too many to be acted upon. What we observed was certainly a microcosm of what is going on all over the country.

Like Toffler, Naisbitt views the initiative process, catapulted into national prominence by the success of Proposition 13 in California, as a citizen demand for a part of the decision-making process. Now in states throughout the country that permit initiatives, voters are launching all kinds of measures; in some states that do not allow such measures, demands are being made to change the constitution.

People pay taxes and are affected by legislation; therefore they cry, We have a right to help make those decisions.

Naisbitt predicts that the schools of the future will experience more taxpayer involvement. Who hasn't seen signs of that already as recall petitions replace school board members in midterm? Gradually legislators are being held accountable for their voting records. Formerly congressmen and senators could come home and tell their constituents anything they wanted to hear, then return to Washington and vote as they pleased. Now voting records and scoreboards are published during each election to verify whether or not a representative really represents us. If one doesn't, we may decide to retire him to private life and send someone to Washington who does.

Our liberal press seldom points out that the conservative gains in the Senate in 1978 and particularly the landslide in 1980, when eleven senators were replaced, followed the vote to give away the Panama Canal. That one issue stirred the voters as nothing I have seen in years. Today the genocide treaty and refusal to defend Central America against Communist expansion may have the same effect.

Naisbitt sees the trend toward participatory involvement

> eventually restructuring all American institutions that serve and employ people. First and foremost, that means corporations.
> All of the present impetus toward making corporations more open and more accountable, the consumer movement, the push for more outside directors, the new shareholder activism, and the trend toward greater employee rights and worker participation originate in the new ethic of participatory democracy.[21]

Finally Naisbitt condemns representative democracy as a tool of the past: "The fact is we have outlived the historical usefulness of representative democracy and we all sense intuitively that it is obsolete. Furthermore, we have grown more confident of our own ability to make decisions about how institutions, including government and corporations, should operate."[22]

Democracy? Really?

While I sympathize with many of Naisbitt's suggestions, I wonder if we really want total democracy. America was founded as a republic, a sharply different form of government. Democracy has historically led to anarchy followed by the rise of a dictatorship. The French Revolution provides a case in point. The cries of "Liberty, equality, fraternity!" led to the death of the king, the founding of a democracy, and a reign of terror when anarchy was rampant, followed by the rise of Napoleon Bonaparte. Russia offers another illustration. The Communist revolution of 1917 led successively to the death of the Czar, democracy, and anarchy, culminating in the rise of another dictator—Vladimir Lenin. Once again the cry for "liberty—freedom" led to revolution, democracy, and anarchy, followed immediately by Communist-style totalitarianism.

To Americans democracy represents the democratic spirit—people expressing themselves through a Constitution, which permits us to elect representatives who legislate on our behalf but who rely on us for reinstatement every two, four, or six years. This system of government may not be perfect, but it has guaranteed more true freedom for more people over a longer period of time than any other form of government. We had better be careful how we tamper with it!

Some of us support constitutional amendments to allow prayer in school, require a balanced budget, or create stronger protections for the rights of the unborn. But even though we fail in our attempts, we still have the freedom to go back to work and try again. While I agree with futurist scholars that we need more citizens' involvement in the governmental process, I am also aware that we must conform to basic constitutional guidelines in order to maintain order and freedom, which is the real purpose of government.

The Death of the Two-Party System

Naisbitt and the futurists foresee the impending death of the two-party system. "The political left and right are dead; all the action is being generated by a radical center," Naisbitt says. He explains that "the two-party system died because people gave up on it. . . . One activist housewife in Chicago summarized the sentiment on the local front: 'They're all alike, Republicans and Democrats. We take them as they come up.'"[23]

Death Notices Premature?

Such statements remind me of the man who was startled one morning when he read his own death notice in his hometown paper's obituary column. The man called to point out the obvious error and offered to make a correction, but he asked if he could write it, much to the chagrin of the columnist. The following appeared in the next day's paper: "I am happy to report that yesterday's announcement of my death in this column was premature—I'm not even sick."

The two-party system may be sick, but it is healing quickly and is far from expiring. True, it almost died! Not many years ago, one couldn't tell a nickel's worth of difference between the liberal Democrats and the "moderate" Republicans. By using the term "moderate," many liberals purposely confused their voting public. Now that Congress votes electronically and the votes can be published in a few hours, it is apparent that "moderate" Republican senators Weicker, Packwood, and others do not vote much differently from liberal Democratic senators Kennedy, Cranston, and Bradley, regardless of the labels used by Dan Rather and his media pals. Political parties previously appeared similar to us because they were!

Now the "conservative megatrend" (which Naisbitt and his futurist friends missed) has begun to gather steam. It is taking over solid control of the Republican party so that conservative Democrats such as Senator Phil Gramm are shifting to the Republican camp. Some ninety-eight southern Democratic state and federal legislators have made or are about to make such defections.

This country is in for a healthy polarization between liberals and conservatives, which will lengthen the life of the two-party system as we know it. Certain shades or degrees of difference will continue, of course, but lines are being drawn on the basis of important issues today. The chart on page 45 shows the contrasting preferences of the two ideologies.

And the list goes on and on. Not all legislators or individuals in either ideology will approve all of these issues, but most will follow a basic line about 80 percent of the time. Otherwise they will have to deceive their constituents in order to get elected. It is unlikely that a 100 percent conservative could get elected in San Francisco or

PREFERENCES OF TWO IDEOLOGIES

LIBERAL	CONSERVATIVE
Big government	Limited government
Welfare state	Individual initiative
Government-controlled economy	Free market, supply & demand
Peace through negotiation	Peace through strength
Perception of Communism as reasonable	Perception of Communism as "an evil empire"
Increased taxes	Lower taxes
Big spending	Reduction of government spending
No fixed moral absolutes	Return to traditional values
Abortion on demand	Pro-life
Increased gay rights	No increase in gay rights
Opposition to prayer in school	Prayer in school
Individual freedom	Individual freedom balanced by individual responsibility
Freedom of speech and press	Freedom of speech and press together with community responsibility
Discontinuance of capital punishment	Capital punishment for capital offenses
Freedom for pornographers	Limitations imposed upon pornographers

Greenwich Village, but it may become increasingly difficult to gain office in the South and other key spots without conservative credentials.

Naisbitt is right—more people are getting involved in the political process and are increasingly demanding more from their representatives than good looks, colorful speeches, and personal charisma. Today's voters, at least conservatives, are becoming informed and voting the issues. Whether the individual is male or female, black or white, Protestant or Catholic makes no difference. The issues have become paramount. For the first time in my life we are seeing conservative Protestants vote for conservative Catholics or for conservative Jews! That has ushered in a whole new megatrend we shall discuss in chapter four.

Megatrend IX: From Hierarchies to Networking

What exactly is networking? you may be wondering. Naisbitt explains this concept quite clearly:

> Simply stated, networks are people talking to each other, sharing ideas, information, and resources. The point is often made that networking is a verb, not a noun. The important part is not the network, the finished product, but the process of getting there—the communication that creates the linkages between people and clusters of people.[24]

Having established my first network (the American Coalition for Traditional Values, which set up 435 congressional district pastor-chairmen for the 1984 election), I was fascinated by this futuristic concept. Networks exist, as Naisbitt says, "to foster self-help, to exchange information, to change society, to improve productivity and work life, and to share resources."[25]

Naisbitt also sees the old pyramid organizational style of management giving ground to the Japanese type of network involvement. In support of this idea he quotes one management expert as warning, "Until we believe that the expert in any particular job is most often the person performing it, we shall forever limit the potential of that person in terms of both his contribution to the organization and his personal development."[26]

One significant benefit is that big business is becoming more interested in the *human beings* that serve as employees. Instead of being viewed as rented bodies on the assembly line, who only do what they are told as fast as they can, employees are being regarded as people and partners, worthy of respect.

Megatrend X: From North to South

The 1980 census bureau statistics reveal that for the first time more Americans live in the South and West than in the North and East. "And it is not news to any American reader that the census of

1980 uncovered a massive shift not just in population but in wealth and economic activity from North to South."[27]

Florida, Texas, and all the southern states have become increasingly attractive. Most of us can identify with the Minnesotan who, after shoveling one hundred thousand tons of snow from 1950 to 1956, moved to California. Whole corporations move or open new plants in the South when favors are offered. I noticed recently that San Diego, a western city, was bidding against ten other areas for a new plant that would hire three thousand workers. The city that won and seven other cities with strong offers were all in the South. Naisbitt finds this shift in population irreversible, and he predicts that it is only the beginning. When I fly over the South, I can't help but notice that plenty of room is available for expansion. As far as economic growth is concerned, Naisbitt chooses Texas, California, and Florida as someday outdistancing all the other forty-seven states combined!

He lists the ten cities of greatest opportunity in the Southwest or West as follows: Albuquerque, Salt Lake, San Antonio, San Diego, San Jose, Tampa, Tucson, Denver, and Phoenix. He overlooked the one that may outstrip them all—Dallas. He lists New York and Chicago as cities that will lose population. It will be interesting to read his next prediction after the 1990 census figures are published.

Naisbitt is quite accurate in his assessment that the population between now and the 21st century will be flowing toward the South and Southwest. If you are looking for a place to launch a new ministry, consider these areas carefully and go where the Holy Spirit leads you (see Col. 3:15).

Megatrend XI: From Either/Or to Multiple Option— The Baskin-Robbins Society

Until the 1960s people made few choices in life. It was an either/ or world, Naisbitt observes:

Father went to work, mother kept house and raised 2.4 children. There were few decisions to make; it was an either/or world:
 • Either we got married or we did not (and of course, we almost always did).

- Either we worked nine to five (or other regular full-time hours) or we didn't work, period.
- Ford or Chevy.
- Chocolate or vanilla.

Admittedly, we sometimes got a third choice: NBC, CBS, or ABC. *Look, Life,* or the *Post.* Strawberry ice cream. But it was still either/or, a society of mass markets and mass market advertising, where homogenized tastes were easily satisfied with few product choices.[28]

Today we live in a market-segmented society—choices, choices, choices. "There are 752 models of cars and trucks sold in the United States"—not counting colors![29] No longer does the traditional family consist of a father who works outside the home, a wife who cares for the home, and their 2.4 children. Now we have two-career families with 1.6 children—or no children—or blended families from previous marriages, unmarried couples, singles, and even communes. Naisbitt suggests that "the basic building block of society is shifting from the family to the individual," and he doesn't believe this multiplicity of family structures will ever revert."[30]

Frankly, I'm not so sure. AIDS, herpes, loneliness, and emptiness may drive more Americans back to traditional values than he thinks. I see the career-woman trend of the late 1970s and early 1980s beginning to peak. An increasing number of success-oriented women find living at the top an empty life-style, and the maternal instinct won't remain dormant.

His suggestion that the nine-to-five workday is not written in stone sounds promising to me. Time is increasingly working for us. Computers and high tech are providing a wave of diversity—not standardization. The "what-is-best-for-the-individual" concept is catching, and there is no telling where it will propel us. I get excited just thinking about life in the 21st century!

STEP TWO

Assess the Values of Today

4

The Born-again Megatrend

The so-called Christian right, powered by TV evangelism, "is destined to become the major social movement in America" during the late 20th century.[1]

Dr. Jeffrey Hadden
Sociologist, University of Virginia

*T*HE most significant force in the past century has not been generated within the field of electronics, the economy, or even government. It is represented by the massive and growing number of born-again Christians, who could exceed 50 percent of the population by the year 2000.

In 1976 an unknown Georgia governor discovered what took the entire nation by surprise. For the first time in over a hundred years, a politician could identify with the born-again Christians of the nation to his advantage. We are told that Jimmy Carter researched the population to see what it would take to become the thirty-ninth president of the United States. To his amazement, one of the six issues deemed most favorable was to identify with the growing born-again segment of the population. That was not difficult for him because, in spite of his liberal political philosophy, he had been a born-again Christian for several years. The experience had a vital impact on his life, and as a Southern Baptist Sunday school teacher, he felt as comfortable with born-again Christians as he did with liberals like Tip O'Neill and Teddy Kennedy.

Consequently he received more votes from born-again Christians than any presidential candidate in this century—except Ronald Reagan, who defeated him in 1980. Many conservative Christian leaders believe that President Carter's most significant contribution during his four-year term of office was to make the term *born-again* respectable. To demonstrate how significant that is, let me tell you about an experience of my own. In 1970 one of the leading publishers of Sunday school literature and church books refused to publish my book, *Revelation Illustrated and Made Plain,* because I would not delete the use of the biblical term, born-again Christians. "It is no longer a meaningful term," I was told. Just one decade later the term helped to elect a president.

The Year of the Evangelical

In 1976 when George Gallup completed the most detailed survey on the religious life of America ever attempted, he discovered at least "45 million 'born-again' Christians" in this nation—and they were growing. This prompted *Time* magazine to designate 1977 as "The Year of the Evangelical" in a cover story. *Time* editors were evidently gripped by the fearsome fact that a single group in America had expanded so significantly (23 percent of the population) that, if it ever became organized and acted in unison, it could easily become the largest voting block in the nation.

Let's put that in perspective. Black Americans (the largest other single group) comprise about 10 percent (20 million people). Homosexuals make up less than 6 percent or about 12 million people. Feminists, in spite of the hype given them by the press, probably represent 1 or 2 percent, and they are losing members. College professors and secular humanists together—including ACLU lawyers—probably don't include more than 6 percent of the population in a nation where 94 percent of the population believe in God.

The elite liberals in media, government, and education (leaders who have manipulated education, entertainment, law, and public opinion throughout most of this century) were struck by the staggering realization that they had a sleeping giant on their hands. If it ever awakened, it could break their strangle hold on the 230 million people of this nation. Surprisingly enough, another three or four years passed before this same realization gripped many Christian leaders.

During the 1930s and 1940s most Christians believed the same dictum my mother taught me: "The country is going down the road to Sodom and Gomorrah morally because that is what the people want." Even as a kid I found that hard to believe (although two years in the air force almost convinced me). But the Gallup Poll on religion and subsequent polls on traditional values awakened the entire country (including the church) to the realization that this nation is not made up of hedonists, pagans, and libertines. Gradually the American people are beginning to realize that many of those in power do not reflect the moral or spiritual values of America: the judges who interpret our laws and bend our Constitution; a number of elected politicians; some of those who write school curricula and determine educational policy; some of those who entertain us on television; those who regularly report (and sometimes distort) the evening news; and many of the journalists who produce our daily papers.

Does the following sound like American hedonism to you? The Gallup Poll discovered that both the churched and the unchurched share many values—not to the same degree, but far more than the media lets on. For example,

- 91 percent would welcome a return to traditional family values;[2]
- 89 percent would welcome more respect and authority in the future;
- 74 percent say they would _not_ like to see more acceptance of drugs;
- 69 percent want more emphasis on hard work;
- 62 percent _oppose_ greater sexual freedom.[3]

While I do not pretend that all America is made up of born-again Christians, I do contend that the nation is not nearly so atheistic and secular as those who control it. Consider this incredible statement from Dr. George Gallup:

If anything, [this] unique study reveals that the unchurched are believers. They pray. They believe in Jesus Christ. They think seriously about life after death. They trust the resurrection story of Easter morning. They want their children to have religious instruction. In fact, with a few variations, the unchurched claim the same turf as the churched—except they are not attending, supporting, or belonging to a congregation of the visible church. One encouraging sign, though, is the fact that more than half express a positive feeling about the institutional religious community.[4]

Spiritual Renewal in the Eighties

"America has begun a spiritual reawakening," said President Ronald Reagan at a Columbus, Ohio, convention in March 1984. Bible study groups are springing up all over the country from suburbia to downtown, from neighborhood homes to business lunchrooms. People who have never studied the Bible before are amazed at its relevance for their lives. Catholics, Baptists, and Episcopalians in some neighborhoods meet together regularly not to fight over doctrinal differences but to learn from God's Word what He wishes to say to them today.

Five years after his famous religious survey, Gallup announced that "Half of the nation's adults (51 percent) say they are more interested in religious and spiritual matters than they were five years ago, according to a 1985 survey. . . ."[5] "Six in 10 Americans believe religion can answer all or most of today's problems while only one person in five clearly doubts the relevance of religion in the modern world."[6]

Christian schools are booming, adding to the over 25,000 that already exist. Giving to churches and church-related ministries increased 11.7 percent—three times the rate of inflation—to over *$31.5 billion* in 1985.

College and high school students show a renewed interest in religious classes; some schools even have waiting lists despite the fact that such subjects have been largely outlawed during the students' educational careers. Dr. Theodore Caplow, chairman of the Sociology Department of the University of Virginia, noted, "In the United States, old-fashioned religion—the religion of a generation ago—is alive and well." He reminded us that 94 percent of Americans believe in God—and at least 60 percent are church members.

Most thoughtful observers acknowledge that, in spite of all the liberal humanist-inspired excess of sexual permissiveness, demands for homosexual rights, drug abuse, child abuse, and pornographic abuse, a vibrant spiritual awakening is occurring in this land. If unchecked by some unforeseen catastrophe, this movement could bring our nation into the 21st century with a moral/spiritual revival like the Great Awakening, which would transform the culture and morals of this land for decades to come. The born-again movement is at the heart of this spiritual renewal.

How Did It All Start?

Spiritually speaking, America was in a sorry state of affairs in the 1930s and 1940s. Church attendance was declining; worldliness became an in-church problem as well as an in-society disease. Franklin Delano Roosevelt's New Deal programs ushered in a welfare-state mentality that caused people to look to government rather than God to supply their needs. Hollywood's producers, writers, and directors used the medium of film to change the moral values of an entire generation. Prohibition was repealed, and a new generation of humanistic gods with Ph.D.'s began to speak authoritatively against God, the Bible, moral absolutes, and religion.

The church became anemic at best, deceived at worst. Liberal theologians began to infiltrate our seminaries, and far too many ministers were educated without confidence in the fundamentals of their faith. Except for an isolated remnant, Christianity was not an appealing faith, and many Christians were intimidated into keeping silent about their faith. Christianity suffered from an intellectual inferiority complex partly caused by outright liberals or Christians who had brought the smug theories of higher criticism from graduate schools into their denominations—the literature, the seminaries, and ultimately the pulpits.

Ministers who survived the onslaught against their faith in seminary and taught the pure, unadulterated Word of God were made to feel like Neanderthal thinkers and social and ecclesiastical extremists rather than faithful servants of God in the tradition of the prophets and apostles. There was no religious persecution—just ostracism. In denominations that moved their pastors at will, many faithful preachers found themselves in small communities where their influence was limited.

Believe it or not, much of this had a purging effect on the church, preparing her for the mighty movement of the Spirit of God that we are experiencing today.

Our Roots

Even during this period of despair and myopic vision, God was still doing His work in bastions of faith like Moody Bible Institute, Bob Jones University, Los Angeles Bible Institute, and other Christian training centers, both inside and outside denominational structures. Other pastors and men of God who were concerned about the liberalism that permeated many of the seminaries also began to found Christian colleges, Bible institutes, and seminaries to ground a future generation of ministers in the fundamentals.

Fundamentalism Splits

In response to the liberalism of this time a tragic rift developed in the ranks of fundamentalism. Some who literally adopted such verses as "Come out from among them and be separate" (2 Cor. 1:17) withdrew from the denominations they identified as liberal. Unfortunately, such decisions were not always made in a spirit of love and concern for the brother of like theology who stayed within his denomination to exercise a positive influence. The test of fellowship among believers became whether or not one withdrew from an "apostate denomination" rather than what another believed about the Bible, the Virgin Birth, or the Second Coming. These splits produced many small, independent churches, which had little affect on society during the next three decades. However, that is rapidly changing because many of those churches have doubled, tripled, and quadrupled in size in the last thirty years and are now becoming involved in the political process.

The Great Leap Forward

The old phrase "Hindsight is better than foresight" certainly applies to the missionary work of the church after the holocaust in

Europe. Over 15 million Americans (many of them Christians) returned to a grateful America after World War II with two major assets: a worldwide vision and the G.I. Bill of Rights. While some of the unchurched embarked on a self-indulgent spree to enjoy things they had been denied during the war, millions of Christian youth enrolled in Christian colleges, Bible institutes, and seminaries. Christian college enrollment skyrocketed, and many schools had to turn young people away.

A few years later, General Douglas MacArthur, our victorious supreme commander in Asia, issued a call for "1,000 missionaries to come to Japan." Although most G.I.'s had sworn that they would never leave American soil again, thousands of them did (for most of their lives) to share the news that our Lord's message "You must be born again!" was not only intended for Americans but for the whole world. Many of the exciting fires of revival now going on in Africa, the Orient, South America, and other continents can be traced to this vintage mission era.

Even as you read these lines, Christian families throughout the country have missionary maps and pictures of missionaries hanging on bulletin boards in their kitchens; these lay people provide an exciting foundation of prayer and financial aid for the nearly 60,000 who have gone to the "uttermost parts of the earth." America has become the greatest launching pad for gospel missions in the history of the world.

Priority on Youth

During the hedonistic period of the thirties and forties, God inspired His servants to launch summer camps—first for high schoolers and then for junior highs and juniors—which had an electrifying impact on the spiritual intensity of our Christian youth. For one or two weeks every year youngsters attended summer camp where they were challenged to serve Christ as ministers, missionaries, or dedicated laymen.

Well do I remember the five summers I spent at a youth camp at a Michigan lake. I gave my life to Christ for the gospel ministry during one of those conferences. In fact, a large percentage of the leaders of today's churches, foreign missions, Christian schools, and parachurch ministries heard God's call at such camps and are now contributing vitally to the Born-again Megatrend. Coincidentally, this chapter is being written from Hume Lake Christian Camp, where I am a frequent speaker and where over 26,000 young people congregate annually.

Youth for Christ and Word of Life

Started just after World War II, Youth for Christ and Word of Life have reached out to millions of young people. Many churches were too small to develop vital youth programs, so these organizations supplied that missing ingredient and were used of God to direct the lives of Christian youth in both Saturday-night programs and a weekday Bible outreach. Campus Life, a division of Youth for Christ, is one of the few Christian witness programs still permitted on some high school campuses. Many unsaved youth have been led to Christ after being invited to a Campus Life meeting by Christian classmates. Young Life and other youth groups, including Jack Wyrtzen's Word of Life in Upper New York, have evangelized thousands during their strategic high school years.

Campus Crusade for Christ International

At the very time that American literacy was at its highest, our educators sent their brightest to Europe to pursue their graduate education. Within two decades American colleges and universities were heavily loaded with professors who had been exposed to the nihilism of Germany's Bonn University, the existentialism of the Sorbonne in Paris, and the European philosophy of rationalism.

Most colleges demand Ph.D. degrees for their faculty members, which supposedly assures a quality education. In actuality, it often ensures that future professors are exposed to an enormous amount of secular humanist training in pursuit of that degree, either in Europe or the United States. And quite a few take their message aggressively into the classroom. In fact, the primary target of the humanists in the 1940s was the 3,000 or more secular colleges and universities of the country.

Even some Christian colleges have been infiltrated by these philosophies. I received a thorough education in humanistic psychology in a fundamental Christian college. How? My professor was a bright young man who had just received his Ph.D. from the University of South Carolina, a graduate program heavily influenced by humanistic professors.

In the late 1940s, Bill Bright, a businessman with a deep burden to reach the world for Jesus Christ, launched a collegiate ministry and started a revolution in sharing one's faith personally. He developed his now famous _Four Spiritual Laws,_ a simplified method of sharing one's faith in Jesus with the intention of leading a person to Christ.

Using the _Four Spiritual Laws_ as his aid, Bill Bright began to lead University of California at Los Angeles (UCLA) students to Christ, discipling them in the Word and evangelism. In one fraternity, Bill led Jerry Riffe, a basketball player and frat house leader, to Christ. Together they targeted the entire fraternity for Christ. Twenty-three accepted the Savior and several entered Christian service.

Word of this phenomenon spread, and soon other campuses were opened to the new movement. Scores of young people began to hear the call of God to dedicate their lives to the college ministry. Bright wisely encouraged each young person to raise his own support, which enabled him to share the responsibility of fund-raising with each member of his staff. Today over 16,000 Campus Crusade for Christ workers are spread across the world, joined by hundreds of thousands of volunteer workers and witnesses.

Like any good work, Crusade was soon joined by many imitators, some of a denominational nature, some sponsored by local churches or other independent groups. Most have used the same basic methods of personal evangelism, Bible study, discipleship, and personal instruction in sharing one's faith. Consequently millions of young people from non-Christian homes have not only received their education but also experienced the life-changing salvation of Jesus Christ. Thousands of these have entered Christian service, and many have returned to lead their parents to Christ.

One case with which I am familiar has been reproduced countless times during the past forty years. A San Diego university professor raised his children in a wholesome way but without interest in spiritual things. His only son was led to Christ through a Campus Crusade worker. The son was then instrumental in leading his mother and two sisters to Christ. Before long the last holdout, his beloved Ph.D. father, got down on his knees, humbly repented, and received the Savior.

Campus Crusade and its many imitators have powerfully impacted the soul harvest that has been going on during the past forty years. Not only have they served as a saving influence on the secular campuses of the nation, but by pursuing the 20–25 percent of the most educated members of society, they also have prepared many of these young people to take positions of influence in our culture.

The full effect of Bill Bright's work has yet to be realized by our society, but it promises to have a powerful impact on the 21st century.

Evangelist Billy Graham

During the past forty years Billy Graham has been the most commanding personality in mass evangelism. He has probably seen more people come to faith in Christ in public meetings than any evangelist in history. Very few churches in America are without members who accepted the Lord in one of his citywide crusades or as a result of his prime-time TV specials. Thousands of children have been reared in Christian families because of his gifted soul-winning ministry.

Like all evangelists, he has faced his share of controversy through the years, first with his fundamentalist brethren over his attempt to evangelize the lost in the mainline churches by including liberal pastors on sponsoring committees. In recent years he has been criticized by conservatives for refusing to take a stand politically and for betraying imprisoned Christians in Communist prisons as he attempted to hold mass evangelistic crusades in Communist countries. Our secular press has not treated him much better than it does other popular religious figures who disagree with it.

The amazing duration of Mr. Graham's ministry has largely been ensured by his personal integrity and consistent faithfulness in exercising his gift as an evangelist for our time. He has lent a dignity and decorum to mass evangelism that have consistently made him one of the most admired men of our time. Today more people are familiar with the term _born again_ and the experience of meeting Christ as Savior than at any time in history.

Evangelism Explosion

The best-kept secret of the thirties and forties was one's personal faith in Christ. Most Christians left soul winning to the pastor and visiting evangelists; therefore, there were no programs, except in Bible schools, to train lay people in evangelism.

Satan couldn't have thought of a better slogan than the popular philosophy of this era: "There are two things you never talk about—religion and politics." Anyone following that axiom today would have little to discuss. Ironically, of course, nothing has greater influence on our lives than religion and politics.

At the same time, the move to the suburbs often took place faster than the churches could be built, and many parents either forsook the habit of attending church or became overly interested in worldly pleasures and activities. Once children came along, the dim roots of their own religious training occasioned slight guilt pangs, which forced them to admit that they were not giving their children any moral instruction.

National evangelist John R. Rice and two pastors of large churches, Jack Hyles and Dr. Lee Robertson, recognized these two phenomena and set about to meet the challenge. They began to travel tirelessly around the country, holding conferences on church evangelism in almost every city in the nation. More than a hundred thousand ministers and millions of lay men and women attended such conferences and were inspired to launch evangelistic programs, often accompanied by "bus ministries."

Used public school buses were purchased inexpensively, and church members combed neighborhoods for miles to find unchurched families with unchurched children. If laymen could not convince Mom and Dad to attend church with the children, they offered to bus the children to church as an alternative.

This combination of soul winning and a bus ministry produced many of the "super churches" of the sixties and seventies. The oil crisis forced these churches to cut back on busing programs for a time, but that did not last long.

One measure of the church growth during the fifties and sixties can be seen in the founding of the Bible Baptist Fellowship denomination, which was established on May 22, 1950, at a meeting of independent Baptist preachers of strong fundamentalist theology and a deep commitment to soul winning.

Today more than 2,700 Baptist Bible Fellowship churches are scattered all across the nation with a membership in the millions. And they are not alone. Several Baptist groups and other denominations have launched new church movements during the past forty years that offer fitting alternatives to the mainline churches, which were disillusioning churchgoers by their drift into liberalism and their lifeless preaching of a dry theology rather than a living relationship with Jesus Christ.

During this same period, the message of a radio gospel preacher challenged D. James Kennedy, an Arthur Murray dance instructor, to accept a personal faith in Christ. Once Kennedy had obtained a seminary degree, he founded the Coral Ridge Presbyterian Church, now the largest church of the PCA denomination in America. Using the soul-winning techniques that had proven successful in his congregation, he then launched a program called Evangelism Explosion in the 1970s to evangelize others who had not been born again. His book of that title became a best seller, and thousands of churches sent their leaders to take his training.

It is almost impossible to exaggerate the impact of these practical training programs. During the first two years after an adult's conversion, it is estimated that he is apt to win half the number of souls he will reach in his lifetime and not just because of his youthful Christian enthusiasm. A converted dentist once explained to me, "When I was first converted, all my friends were pagans. But by the time I was two years old in the Lord, I was surrounded by Christians."

The Gallup Poll of 1980 revealed that 25 million people had shared their faith with another for the purpose of leading him or her to Christ, and a whopping 5 million claimed to do so once a week. Bill Bright and Dr. D. James Kennedy have together trained more individuals to share their faith than any two men since the days of the apostle Paul. As a result, Christianity is no longer a private matter. Personal evangelism flourishes in the best tradition of the evangelistic church of the first century.

The Bill Gothard Phenomenon

In the early 1970s Bill Gothard began a series of week-long studies called Basic Youth Conflicts to resolve the "generation gap" that existed between parents and their children. As part of the course every person was given a four-pound red notebook, which contained Gothard's notes and enabled each person to refer to his principles from then on.

In some of the major cities in the country, attendance went as high as 25,000 people. Gradually his institute was taken by millions of people. All over America confessions of wrongdoing and requests for forgiveness brought estranged individuals back together. Thousands of people are enjoying a more harmonious life today because they attended a Gothard seminar.

Other seminars for youth, married couples, athletes, and business people sprang up and have positively impacted the many who have attended. But none has come close to equaling the Gothard phenomenon.

Expository Preaching Related to Life

American fundamentalism was born out of evangelism and a heavy emphasis upon the preaching of sin, salvation, and judgment. For many years it did not progress far from those themes, which the apostle Paul called the "milk" of the Word. Paul challenged individuals to study the Word so as to have their "senses exercised to discern both good and evil" (Heb. 5:14).

If people had listened to his advice, liberalism might not have crept into many denominations during the first half of this century.

The pendulum began to swing back once emphasis was again placed on Bible teaching and exposition in place of topical or textual sermons.

I would be remiss not to mention the name of Dr. Harry A. Ironside, long-time pastor of the Moody Memorial Church of Chicago. Not only was he equipped with a deep, sonorous voice, but he also possessed an almost photographic memory coupled with a practical outlook on life.

Dr. Ironside visited many of the preacher training colleges of the nation as well as the great Bible conferences that attracted large crowds. He used 2 Timothy 3:16 to emphasize the inspiration of the Bible, often stressing that Scripture was to be "profitable" or practical in the life of the believer. Consequently he became a role model for many of today's pastors who are known for practical sermons based on a faithful exposition of the Word of God. Another powerful influence on in-depth preaching in this country has been Dallas Theological Seminary. Dedicated to equipping preachers with a thorough knowledge of the Word of God and the ability to make it relevant to today's hearers, that institution is responsible for a large number of today's growing churches.

As preaching became more interesting and practical, the super churches of the 1960s, built primarily on evangelism and bus ministries, gradually were replaced by the Bible-teaching churches, some of which have experienced incredible growth. One illustration is the great Belleview Baptist Church of Memphis, Tennessee, pastored for many years by Dr. R. G. Lee, who may go down in history as the greatest American orator ever. His successor is my good friend Dr. Adrian Rogers, an exceptional Bible teacher and preacher, considered by some of his pastoral colleagues to be "the best preacher in America." Under his leadership, the Memphis church holds three morning services and has purchased 365 acres of land just outside the Memphis city line. When the new church complex is opened for worship, 6,000 to 12,000 worshippers will be able to gather in one place, and the old building will be sold to another growing church.

Prestonwood Baptist Church in North Dallas, Texas (where I serve as an associate pastor and teach an adult Bible class satellited to more than 150 churches each Sunday morning) is pastored by Dr. Billy Weber. It has probably experienced the most explosive growth of any church in America. Today it is not uncommon to see 5,000 people gathered to worship there on Sundays. Pastor Weber, one of the most amazing ministers I have ever known, expects the congregation _to double in size in five years._

Such church growth may be unusual, but it is increasing. A Charlotte church has just purchased 100 acres under the leadership of Dr. Ross Rhodes, another superb Bible teacher. Second Baptist Church of Houston recently completed a thirty-million-dollar expansion program.

In the 1960s and 1970s most large cities featured at least one church auditorium, with 1,800 to 2,500 seats. Today in many cities we can identify several auditoriums with 3,000 to 6,000 seats and with two and sometimes three morning services. Some 10,000-seat churches are currently under construction.

As we look across America, we will find Bible-teaching centers of all denominations, including Southern Baptists, Presbyterians, charismatics, and many independents. In view of the fact that our Lord addressed crowds estimated in excess of 20,000, there seems no limit to a church's potential size. If God continues to bless his ministry, I would not be surprised to see Dr. Jerry Falwell build a 25,000-seat auditorium on his 2,500-acre site in Lynchburg, Virginia, before the year 2000.

Looking down the road to the future, I foresee no diminution in church growth—barring a total secular takeover of local, state, and national governments. If that happens, the awesome power of government could be used to stifle church growth by refusing needed building permits for church expansion.

The Proliferation of Bible Translations

When I was a boy, it was not unusual to hear someone say in exasperation, "I have a hard time understanding the Bible." Happily, that is no longer a valid complaint. Although the King James Bible was unrivaled for beauty of expression and accuracy in its day, we must remember that it was translated in 1611. Language has changed drastically in 350 years, and many twentieth century readers cannot understand or gain much from its Renaissance language.

Although many translations appeared in the first half of the twentieth century, notably the American Standard Version of 1911, none really attracted widespread use. But after World War II, when the nation's appetite for Bible reading and study began to increase, a number of new translations became available for Protestant churches: the New American Standard Version, the Berkeley Bible, The Amplified Bible, the Revised Standard Version, the New International Version, the more recent New King James Version, and for the Catholic church, the Confraternity Edition. More Americans are reading their Bibles today than ever before, and none seems to be read more frequently than The Living Bible, a paraphrase written by Ken Taylor for his ten children to use in their daily devotions. Today more than 30 million copies are in print, and it is being translated into hundreds of foreign languages.

Since the printed page is the method God chose to communicate with man in the first place, we can conclude that it is the best means possible for men and women to know God personally. Although we can only guess at the number of people who read the Bible, the Gallup Poll discovered that 15 percent of the population read the Bible "every day," and the number who read it occasionally or who turn to the Bible for help in moments of crisis rises graphically to as high as "76 percent." Only "about 24 percent never read the Bible." Without question, the Bible is the most influential book in America.

The Christian School Movement

Modern history books do not tell the real story of what made this nation the most prosperous on record. It certainly wasn't our size, natural resources, or national origin. No, we grew in maturity and strength because our forefathers determined to educate every man's child, not just the rich or the royal-blooded as in the European system—and that educational system was based on the Word of God. Thus we developed the highest literacy rate in history. Most citizens read the Bible and knew its principles for living, whether or not they were Christians. It should be pointed out that the humanists had nothing to do with that high literacy rate but had everything to do with its demise.

For 200 years (from 1636 to 1837) most children were educated at home or in private or religious schools. Not until Robert Owen, the atheist socialist, gathered together free thinkers, Unitarians, and transcendentalists in what he called the Friends of Education was there a concerted attempt to establish public schools at the taxpayer's expense. His purpose was to alter the philosophy of the next generation. It took almost 150 years for Horace Mann, John Dewey, and their Unitarian and secular humanist philosophy to so dominate public education that in many parts of the country it is no longer fit for the children of Christian parents.

When that fact became painfully clear after World War II, churches and interested Christians in the early 1950s began to establish Christian schools as an extension of their church ministries. But the Supreme Court decision in 1962 resulting in the elimination of prayer and the curtailing of Bible reading in public schools the next year probably did more to ignite the Christian school movement than any other single factor. During the 1970s three new Christian schools were founded every day.

In 1970 Donald Howard introduced Accelerated Christian Education (ACE) schools of Dallas, Texas. Instead of mandating one teacher per grade for twenty to thirty-five students, he instituted a curriculum that almost any educated person could administer, allowing the students to study at their own pace. Equipped with lesson books, cassettes, and other materials in an individual learning center, a church of almost any size can afford to sponsor a Christian school. It is estimated that one-fifth of all Christian schools today use the ACE program.

During the late 1970s and 1980s, another phenomenon, also inspired by parental dissatisfaction with our secular schools, has spread like wildfire across the educational landscape: home education. Currently almost 2 percent of all students are educated at home, 14 percent in Christian or private schools, and about 84 percent in our government-controlled public schools. At their present rate of growth, that should increase to 5 percent for home schooling and 30 percent for private education before the year 2000 (if we do not elect a liberal president who will take control of a child's education and give it to the educators of humanism).

Dr. Paul Kienel, president of the Association of Christian Schools

International (ACSI), asserts from recent figures that some 25,000 Christian schools (with an average size of 125 students) exist in America in 1986. Using these figures, we arrive at a figure of 3,125,000 students enrolled in Christian schools. Therefore, of the 45,000,000 students enrolled in schools nationwide, the Christian schools represent approximately 7 percent of our nation's students. Another 7 percent attend other private schools.

On the average, students in Christian schools are one year and four months ahead of their peers in public education. ACSI Christian schools use the Stanford Achievement Test, the most difficult of the achievement tests, for their comparison with the national norm (which is established by the public schools). This means that upon graduation from eighth grade, the average Christian school student is on a par with a public school sophomore into the fourth month of his school year.

The current growth rate for Christian schools (three new schools each day) is about 1,095 each year. Even if one out of every three were to fail, we will still have some 10,220 new Christian schools by the year 2000.

When we consider the future of Christian education, we must consider what our elected officials might do to education during the next decade. If conservatives are elected, they will probably put the responsibility for education back into the hands of the parents and give them some kind of tax relief so they will not have to support both public and private education during the lives of their children. This relief would accelerate the development and growth of all kinds of private education. On the other hand, if the liberals regain total control of our federal government, you can be sure they will do everything in their power to limit the choice in education to one controlled by the secular humanists of education and the powerful National Education Association (NEA) instead of parents. The reason for this? Both groups believe Abraham Lincoln's maxim—that the philosophy controlling today's classroom will control tomorrow's government.

This amazing growth in Christian schools during the past two decades means that Christians are developing some effective leaders who see the world from God's viewpoint, not the humanist world view. Christian school students also score well on college entrance exams, according to Dr. Kienel. On the other hand the education system at large has produced 23 million adults who are functionally illiterate, according to a 1975 study.[7]

Dr. Kienel also indicates that a much higher percentage of young people go to college to prepare for the ministry and the mission field from Christian schools than from the public sector. Through these Christian schools, we are helping to prepare the leaders of the future—both secular and sacred.

The Burgeoning Creationist Movement

Keeping pace with and emanating from the same roots as the Born-Again Megatrend (late 1930s and 1940s) has come the Creationist Movement. It has been purposely ignored by the humanistic media and academic community for fear it would disprove several of their basic lies: (1) that evolution is a fact; (2) that all scientists are evolutionists; (3) that there is no scientific evidence for creation, thus no creator—no God; and (4) that since there is no God, there are no moral absolutes.

Some courageous scientists loudly disagree with these theories, despite the evolutionists' tendency to belittle their academic credibility. The most vocal is Dr. Henry M. Morris, sometimes called "Mr. Creation." Dr. Morris earned his Ph.D. in hydraulics at the University of Minnesota and for thirteen years chaired the Department of Civil Engineering at Virginia Polytechnic Institute, the third largest engineering school in the nation.

In the early 1960s he and a number of creationist scientists, each with at least one graduate degree in a science field, founded the Creation Research Society, which today numbers among its 2,700 members at least 700 scientists with postgraduate degrees in pure or applied natural science. All believe in the deity of Jesus Christ, the historicity of the Genesis record, and a worldwide cataclysmic flood. Dr. Morris became the first president of the Creation Research Society and for many years inspired thousands of scientists to be outspoken against the false claims of evolution as science. His books—*The Twilight of Evolution, The Troubled Waters of Evolution, Scientific Creationism*, and many others—have had a profound impact on the thinking of both scientists and impressionable youth who previously had been led to believe that evolution was the only credible explanation for man's origin.

In 1970 it was my privilege along with Dr. Arthur L. Peters and Dr. Morris to co-found Christian Heritage College of San Diego, California. In 1972 under Dr. Morris's leadership the college launched the Institute for Creation Research, which today numbers a staff of over thirty individuals who have produced millions of pieces of literature and over sixty books exposing the unsupported theories of "evolutionary science." Together with Dr. Duane Gish and other scientists on the staff, they have debated world-renowned evolutionists on their own university turf, proving that evolution is not a fact and that scientific creationism is just as credible a theory of man's origin and therefore worthy of equal consideration in school curricula.

In 1985 a panel of fifteen judges considered the question of whether or not scientific creationism should be taught in public schools. Seven voted to include creationism, only one vote short of acceptance. I predict that before the end of this decade the efforts of Dr. Morris and his growing army of creation scientists will finally be rewarded with academic acceptance for creationism as an alternate theory in public school texts.

Creationism is important in this recap of the Born-again Megatrend because it further substantiates the depth of this movement's impact on our society. The movement not only elicits a spiritual response from millions of souls to a theological message but directly influences the intellectual and academic area—even that of science, long thought the special domain of the secularists. Thanks to Dr. Morris and his creationist colleagues, it is now possible for scientists to heed God's challenge to "reason together."

The Booming Christian Book Business

Almost seven thousand Christian bookstores throughout the nation make available the bulk of the one-billion-dollars worth of Christian books and related literature sold in the country each year. The secular stores either discriminate against evangelical books or simply don't see the need to carry them. The secular market tends to introduce many books for short-term sale and allows them to go out of print unless they become instant best sellers. Christian books often possess a much longer life.

During the past twenty years I have watched the Christian book industry grow to at least ten times larger than when I came out with my first book in 1966. By the time this book is published, close to 8 million of my fledglings will have seen the light of day—and I am only one communicator. Hundreds of Christian authors are influencing millions of people through the printed page.

The Sunday school curriculum has also become a more effective communicator of God's truth in the past forty years. This Bible-based material, which has inspired millions of students to study the Word of God, has created the highest biblical literacy level we have ever experienced inside the church. By contrast, the humanistically controlled public sector of education has declined in learning.

The Christian publishing business has had a profound impact upon the religious awakening within this country during the past century. It promises to provide the major reading material of the born-again movement during the next century.

Personal evangelism, expository preaching, new translations of the Bible, Christian education, and Christian publishing have all contributed to the Born-again Megatrend. But by far the most visible factor is the electric church because of its wide outreach to millions in this country and abroad.

The Birth of the Electric Church

When radio became a household appliance, several men of God stepped out by faith to claim the airwaves for the Lord. One such stalwart was Dr. Charles E. Fuller, a resonant-voiced Bible teacher who launched the "Old-Fashioned Revival Hour" in 1932. One of the thousands who first heard the gospel on this program was Jerry Falwell, who remembers his mother's listening to this program each day. Fuller was followed by Dr. M. R. DeHaan of the "Radio Bible Class" and several others.

Percy Crawford not only inaugurated a national radio program but also became the first to build a totally Christian radio station—a concept that has burgeoned into almost *one thousand* Christian radio stations today (out of nearly nine thousand stations in the nation). Hardly a city or town exists in our country that does not have religious programming. Literally millions of souls have come to faith in Christ through Christian radio, and millions more have been renewed and grounded in the faith by their favorite radio preachers, from Dr. Charles E. Fuller to Dr. DeHaan to Dr. James Dobson.

Television

Television is the most powerful communication vehicle ever invented. Its potential for preaching the gospel was not lost on aggressive Christian leaders, such as Dr. R. G. Lee and other local pastors who began telecasting their morning services into the homes of the unchurched or shut-ins who would otherwise miss a morning worship experience. During the sixties several Christian radio stations obtained television licenses and also began TV ministries.

For the first three decades of television, Sunday morning was such unpopular air time that the only ones who bought it were churches. Consequently, millions of Americans who rarely or never went to church were able to worship with the church of their choice, ranging from formal to casual, from Baptist to charismatic. Televised church services have not only confronted millions of individuals with the claims of Christ, but they have also broadened all Christians' understanding of denominations other than their own.

Incredible Growth

The "electric church" now commands an enormous audience. A recent Nielsen rating found that Pat Robertson and Jimmy Swaggart are reaching between 7 and 8 million people every week. Those significant statistics make these men and telecasters like Jerry Falwell, D. James Kennedy, and Charles Stanley the greatest soul winners in the nation.

"More than 33 million households, 40.2 percent of all homes in the United States, watched at least one of 10 television preachers for at least six minutes once a month," according to a 1985 Nielsen study. Nielsen spokesman William Behanna said this audience compares to the "most top-rated network, prime time shows," which also reach about 40 percent of U.S. viewers.[8] Quite a mission field!

Today we can point to a hundred Christian television stations and four Christian-owned cable TV networks, one of which, Pat Robertson's Christian Broadcasting Network (CBN), is cabled into over 34 million homes.

Soon direct-broadcast satellite capabilities will enable Americans to bring three or four Christian networks into their homes. They will no longer need to watch secular TV programs, the steady diet of sex and violence that has caused millions of viewers to turn off the tube.

One indicator of television's effectiveness can be seen in the fact that charismatic churches are growing at a faster rate than noncharismatic churches. Charismatics early forecasted the potential of television evangelism, and today they outnumber noncharismatic programmers by ten to one (over eighty-five charismatic programmers of weekly shows to fewer than seven national noncharismatic producers).

The daily television shows and all four Christian cable networks are controlled by charismatics. Their style of worship lends itself to television, and their people are sacrificially generous and support the costs of TV production. Their dominant presence on television could help to account for the Gallup survey's indication that charismatics cross all denominational lines. Seven million Roman Catholics claim to be charismatic and born again, together with many Episcopalians, Baptists, Methodists, and members of other faiths.

Gallup says the "35 million evangelicals" he identified in his poll share three major distinctions: (1) they are born again, (2) they have shared their faith with someone else, and (3) they accept the Bible literally. Another 34 million claim to be born again, but lack one of the other qualifiers. According to the Gallup and other surveys, the evangelical church is experiencing rapid growth, again validating the influence of television on the religious life of the country since most Christian TV programmers advocate those three characteristics.

Just last Sunday I heard a Baptist deacon testify that his wife received Christ while watching a television program and began to attend a local church only two weeks later with their daughter. Before a month had passed, he decided to attend with them—and was converted within two weeks.

Criticism of the Electric Church

Liberal churchmen have attacked the electronic church of TV and radio as being a deterrent to church growth. Actually, the opposite is true for Bible-believing churches. However, at the same time that evangelical churches are growing, liberal churches are experiencing their greatest decline. Could it be that the programmers who faithfully teach the Bible on TV and radio create a hunger in the hearts of people to attend a church that proclaims the same Bible-based message?

The Gallup Polls certainly do not indicate that the electronic church has detracted from church growth. Studies suggest that the impersonal nature of a televised church service only serves as a supplement to the spiritual diet of many Christians. I believe that the God who commanded us not to "forsake the assembling of yourselves together" has put a yearning in our hearts for community worship.

Gallup notes that his 1984 survey, taken jointly by the Annenberg School of Communication and the Gallup organization, proves that religious television not only does not cut into church attendance but is needed to offset the secular influence of commercial television. Consequently, he challenges the denominations to get into religious programming—and to stop complaining about those who are presently developing it.

The media love to trumpet the fact that about $1 billion is raised annually by TV evangelists. Naturally, they find something sinister in such fund-raising. However, they almost never mention that most of this money goes to pay the exorbitant airtime costs set by the networks. Nor do they point out that the production costs of TV ministries reach into the millions of dollars.

While media liberals are quick to criticize TV ministries, they never censure pornographers like Hugh Hefner and Larry Flint for the $10-billion-a-year pornographic trade that has such a demoralizing effect on our nation. The media simply hates the electric church because they disagree with its message.

Fifty-two Percent of the Population by 2000 A.D.?

My suggestion that over 50 percent of our population could report a born-again experience by the 21st century has been regarded as cavalier at best and preposterous at worst. But the 1985 Gallup Report on *Religion In America* during the past fifty years (from 1935, the first year such polls were made) shows a 6 percent increase in the number of born-again Christians since 1976. During that time our number grew from 34 percent of the adult population to 40 percent in 1984. If we continue at the same rate during the next sixteen years, that number will stand at 52 percent when we enter the 21st century. And with all of the above reasons for our past growth to continue, plus many others we do not have space to include, that number could even be higher.

The Born-Again Megatrend has certainly had a powerful influence on the last half of the twentieth century. If evangelical Christians work with the Conservative Megatrend, which we will examine in the next chapter, they may have an even greater influence on the next century.

5

The Conservative Megatrend

The Conservative Revival will go on for half a century!

Russell Kirk
Conservative Intellectual Author

The Mind of a Conservative

THE landslide victory given President Ronald Reagan in 1984 was not just a rejection by the American people of the liberalism that had dominated our country for fifty years. It demonstrated the growing conservative mood that has been building for over two decades and has become almost a tidal wave—in other words, the Conservative Megatrend.

Just over twenty years ago, in 1964, the disastrous defeat of presidential candidate Senator Barry Goldwater showed the impotence of the conservative movement and the awesome power of liberalism in this country. Not only the White House but both the Senate and the House of Representatives were controlled by liberals. To make matters worse, there were so many liberal Republicans in Congress and so few conservative Democrats that of the 537 federal office holders, fewer than 25 percent were deemed conservatives. Yet polls indicated that nearly two-thirds of the American people considered themselves to be conservative.

This dilemma can be attributed largely to the fact that in 1964 liberals almost totally dominated the media. Except for the *Man-*

chester Leader, few newspapers anywhere endorsed Senator Goldwater. Virtually no newscaster on the autocratically liberal networks of NBC, CBS, or ABC was even kind to the Arizona senator, much less unbiased. The American people did not reject Barry Goldwater; they repudiated the characterization of a warmonger fashioned by the media.

This was the first election in history that used TV commercials to destroy the reputation of a great American. He was projected as a trigger-happy monster whose finger could not be trusted near the atomic "hot button" at the White House. Then California Governor Edmund "Pat" Brown, a liberal, uttered the classic statement that characterized the effects of the vicious TV commercials: "I smell the stench of Nazism. I hear the march of storm troopers." Other liberals compared Goldwater to Adolph Hitler—in spite of the fact that he is part Jewish. Since 1964 twenty years of faithful service in the U.S. Senate have proved the inaccuracy of those charges, but they accomplished their purpose and elected the very liberal Lyndon Baines Johnson, whose "Great Society" plunged this nation into a deficit spending cycle from which it may never recover.

In those days there was no Christian cable television network to educate over 22 million Americans weekly. There was no Cable News Network (CNN) that sometimes tried to be objective, and very few newsletters used direct mail to educate special interest groups concerning the socialistic results of the liberal decisions made by our elected leaders. There was no Moral Majority, New Right, Religious Right, Concerned Women for America, among organizations that in recent years have succeeded in awakening a vast army of Americans.

In fact, few of us back then dreamed that America would ever experience a conservative revival. Most knowledgeable conservatives considered it just a matter of time before our country would become so socialized that it could merge with the Soviet Union into the socialist world envisioned by the Council on Foreign Relations and other one-worlders.

Fortunately, both secular conservatives, anti-Communists, and Christian conservative leaders refused to give up. They began to work tirelessly toward the re-establishment of the traditional values upon which this country was originally founded. Their work is far from complete, but their progress is much greater than many of them dreamed twenty years ago. Although we cannot relate the entire story in one chapter, it is so vital to the future of America that we must pause to include a synthesis of it here.

A Choice, Not an Echo?

Prior to 1964 politics in America was overwhelmingly controlled by liberals in both parties. In the 1940s and 1950s there was very little difference between Republican and Democratic candidates. On the federal level, a vote for a Democrat represented a vote for an extremely liberal to liberal-moderate candidate (except in the South). A Republican vote usually identified a candidate midway between a liberal and a liberal moderate. Only a few conservatives made it to Washington.

The reason is not difficult to ascertain. Most congressmen are lawyers, and the legal profession has been dominated by more liberals than any other profession. Just as John Dewey and his disciples successfully secularized our once-great public school system, so Supreme Court justices Oliver Wendell Holmes, Louis Brandeis, Felix Frankfurter, Earl Warren, and William O. Douglas and judges at other levels secularized our courts and legal system. When we add a liberal domination of journalism and the Hollywood and Broadway liberal mentality, which usurped the television industry in the early 1950s, we can understand how the liberal troika of education, government, and media dominated America from 1930 to 1980—contrary to the conservative yearnings and beliefs of the American people.

Abraham Lincoln once said, "The philosophy of the public schools of one generation will be the philosophy of government in the next generation." Had it not been for the church and the Born-again Megatrend discussed in the last chapter, as well as the many conservative groups, publications, and individuals that came to life in the late 1950s and early 1960s, that would certainly be true today. Remember, Lincoln uttered his pronouncement before the age of television.

Ted Turner once told me, "I believe television is the most powerful force in America!" I replied, "Ted, what about government? It makes our laws." To this he responded, "But television elects the government!"

For that reason the liberal troika had almost complete control of America before 1980. And that is why they have invariably cried, "Fascist, Nazi, extremist, Ayatollah," or worse whenever they heard the names Goldwater, Ronald Reagan, Jerry Falwell, Jesse Helms, Pat Robertson, and other conservative, law-abiding Americans whom they perceive as a threat to total liberal control of our country.

Liberals fear competition. They oppose it fiercely in education, and that is why the public schools and the National Education Association (NEA) fight so determinedly against Christian schools, home schooling, and tuition tax credits. ABC and NBC were terrified by even the suggestion that Jesse Helms might be successful in his attempt to take over CBS. One family-oriented TV network that provided clean and wholesome programming with an unbiased presentation of the news would break the monopoly of the networks which has enabled them to produce the filth they sadistically call entertainment. (If Helms is successful, they may all have to clean up their act.)

Back to Goldwater and 1964

The fact that 27 million Americans voted for Senator Goldwater suggested that America was not a liberal-socialist nation of hedonists. But almost two more decades would pass before liberalism's idealistic programs would expose themselves for the socialistic frauds they really were. The federal deficit continually increased from under $317 million in 1964 to nearly $834 million in 1979,[1] a fact which produced a despair and hopelessness in this country not evident since the Great Depression. That 27 million voters could see through the distortions of the media and still vote for Goldwater in 1964 gave me hope—and not to me only but to thousands of other conservatives.

The next day I did something I had never done before. As the pastor of a growing and influential church in San Diego, I penned a letter to actor Ronald Reagan, commending him for the outstanding speeches he had made during the Goldwater campaign and urging him to run for governor of California in 1966. I reminded the president of that letter during a visit to the White House in 1985. He graciously thanked me, and one of his aides later told me that mine was one of about 11,000 similar letters he received after the Goldwater debacle.

In March 1985, the president thanked Dr. LaHaye for his efforts to strengthen the family and for suggesting what the president could do to help the families of the nation.

Although America's conservative revival received its "great leap forward" during the Goldwater campaign, its roots can be traced to the basic conservative beliefs of its citizens, both religious and secular, emanating from World War II. Then came the anti-Communist movement of the late fifties and early sixties. Liberals like to identify anti-Communists as extremist crazies or "McCarthyites," whereas most were just concerned citizens who viewed Communism as a totalitarian movement bent on world conquest. Many organizations produced books and pamphlets, which educated millions of our citizens to the dangers of the Soviets, Communism, and the United Nations. Such names as J. Edgar Hoover (director of the FBI), Cleon Skousen (author of *The Naked Communist* and a former FBI agent), Dr. Fred Schwartz (founder of the Christian Anti-Communist League), Robert Welch (founder of the John Birch Society), and anti-Communist radio broadcasters Carl McIntire, Dean Manion, and Dan Smoot produced a creditable Anti-Communist campaign.

Today some of their disciples have started grassroots movements that, although woefully underfinanced, are actually more effective than the liberal troika of education, government, and media, in spite of their access to almost limitless amounts of federal money. The principal target is a registered, informed, and voting electorate. The conservative movement assumes that when enough Americans understand the issues and know where each candidate stands on them, they will vote on principles first, party or personality later. That is becoming more true with each passing election and is the key to fulfilling Russell Kirk's prediction that "the Conservative Revival will go on for half a century."

Dr. Fred Schwartz—1956

While pastoring a growing church in the suburbs of Minneapolis (which still has one of the most liberal daily newspapers in the nation), I was invited to a ministers' breakfast to hear a Christian medical doctor from Australia, Dr. Fred Schwartz. I can still remember his three basic points of Marxism: 1) atheism, 2) evolution, and 3) economic determinism. I was startled when he added, "These are the three basic tenets of the American public school system!"

Nine years later, after moving to a pastorate in California, I started a Christian high school because I realized we were losing the battle for the minds of our youth. In 1980 Dr. Schwartz's insights and a subsequent reading of Dr. Francis Schaeffer's books inspired me to declare war on secular humanism, the fundamental heresy underlying Marxism, socialism, and liberalism.

Dr. Schwartz, who later founded the Christian Anti-Communist

League, has awakened millions to the threat of world communism. In fact, many of his predictions of Communist takeovers in Asia, Africa, and Central America have come true. From August 28–31, 1961, Dr. Schwartz succeeded miraculously in getting network TV to air four one-hour anti-Communist specials—commercially sponsored presentations of evening sessions of James Colbert's Southern California School of Anti-communism, a seminar held at the Los Angeles Sports Arena. They featured Senator Thomas Dodd, Congressman Walter Judd, and other fearless anti-Communists. Following this event, the networks refused to sell commercial television time for these anti-Communist programs.

In 1958 the most controversial figure to appear on the scene in the past forty years (except for Senator Joseph McCarthy), wealthy candy manufacturer Robert Welch, founded the John Birch Society. Named after a Southern Baptist missionary who was murdered by the Communists as they took over China, it has alerted and educated additional millions of citizens. Upon his death in 1985, the Birch Society could point to chapters in every city in the country, a library of anti-Communist books printed into the millions of copies, a very effective speaker's bureau, and thousands of members who have taken their place in government, education, medicine, law, the ministry, and many other fields of influence. Many leaders of today's conservative movement have been influenced to one degree or another by the literature, teachings, or conferences produced by the society.

After watching its growth from a distance these past twenty-five years, I still cannot understand why a patriotic, anti-Communist organization, which has harmed no one, is not subversive, and has never advocated the overthrow of the government by force and violence, could be so consistently hated by our liberal press and media. "Birchers" have been stigmatized as "Fascists," "Nazis," "Ayatollahs," and worse. But then, so have many of us on the religious or conservative right who have called for a return of our country to traditional values. What do we all have in common? Apparently we pose a threat to the overwhelming liberal control in government, education, and media.

"You Are What You Read"

Technology in the 1960s was controlled primarily by liberals. Printing presses, magazine publishers, radio, television, and wire services were utilized by them to fill the minds of the people. Thomas Paine was right, "The pen is mightier than the sword"— and we were being led to an accommodation with socialism by the wielding of liberal pens.

Time, Newsweek, and *Life* have been extremely popular throughout most of my lifetime—and very liberal. Most cities have boasted two newspapers—both liberal. Unless an individual subscribed to *Human Events, U.S. News & World Report* (when David Lawrence was the publisher), *National Review,* or someone's newsletter (like *The Dan Smoot Report*), he hardly knew what was really happening to our nation.

The media romance with the United Nations (dominated by the Soviets since day one) is evidenced by their reluctance to criticize any of its agencies until just the last few years when its Marxist prejudice and personal excesses were impossible to disguise. People know it cannot be trusted to work in our best national interest. Where did they get their information? From conservative and anti-Communist literature.

William F. Buckley, Jr.

One of the pioneers of the conservative movement who has used both print media and television to communicate his message to the American people is the brilliant William F. Buckley, Jr. My friend, Richard Viguerie, in his book *The New Right: We're Ready To Lead,* paid him this tribute:

William F. Buckley, Jr., has played so many roles it's hard to name them all: Editor of *National Review,* the conservative intellectual journal for 25 years. Syndicated columnist since 1962 whose witty commentary has kept liberals off balance year after year. Host of the weekly TV program *Firing Line* since 1966, the only regular conservative show on the nation's most important mass medium. Author of a dozen-plus best-selling books, both fiction and non-fiction. *God and Man at Yale* was published almost 30 years ago, in 1951. It was a literary shot heard around the nation, if not the world.

Less well known, I'm sure, have been Bill Buckley's many organization contributions to the conservative movement. Young Americans for Freedom was founded at his family's Sharon, Conn., home in 1960. Over the next two years he helped the Conservative Party of New York, which has played such a decisive role in electing dozens of conservatives to the state legislature and the U.S. Congress.

Bill Buckley himself ran for mayor of New York City in 1965 in a memorable campaign. His effort is probably best remembered for his wisecrack response when he was asked what he would do if he won: "Demand a recount."

But in fact, in that race and elsewhere he proposed a number of sensible programs, prompting him later to write a small but important book, *Four Reforms,* which touched on welfare, taxes, crime and education.

Bill was a major figure in the 1964 founding of the American Conservative Union, which alone carried much of the organizational burden of the right until the mid-70's when New Right groups like The Conservative Caucus, the Committee for the Survival of a Free Congress and the National Conservative Political Action Committee were formed. He also worked closely with a number of anti-communist organizations in the 1950s and 1960s, including probably the best known of all—the Committee of One Million (Against the Admission of Communist China to the United Nations).

It was Bill Buckley's unique contribution to draw together, basically through *National Review,* three kinds of conservatives in America. As outlined by George Nash in his definitive book, *The Conservative Intellectual Movement in America,* they were:

• The "classical liberals" or libertarians, who resisted the threat of government to liberty, free enterprise and the individual, including men like Frank Chodorov and John Chamberlain.

• The "new conservatives" or "traditionalists," who urged a return to traditional religious and ethical standards, including men like Russell Kirk and Richard Weaver.

• The militant anti-communists, who believed that the West was engaged in a deadly struggle with communism, including men like Whittaker Chambers and James Burnham.

The New Right owes much of what we believe in and are fighting for to such outstanding men and the catalyst who brought them together, William F. Buckley, Jr.[2]

The books and articles of William Buckley and many other men have influenced me and other conservatives. I have listed a few at the end of this chapter.

What Is the New Right?

The term *New Right* was first used in the early 1960s to describe the rising tide of conservative college young people, many of whom have become today's political activists, organizational heads, politicians, and writers of the Conservative Megatrend. We know they must be "the good guys" because the liberal establishment media speak so disparagingly of them.

They are not really new, of course; their conservative philosophy just seems new to the millions of individuals who have been exposed to liberalism from kindergarten through graduate school and whose only news source is TV, the daily liberal newspaper, or the popular weekly magazine. In reality, conservatism is as old as America.

The New Right is made up of conservative people who are comfortable with religion and its moral values. They are Catholics, Protestants, and Jews with a love for America, family life, and free enterprise with minimum governmental control. Most consider communism the number one threat to world peace and agree with President Reagan, who called the Soviets "an evil empire."

The New Right represents "the silent Americans" of the 1950s and 1960s who are no longer silent. As long as they lived quietly in this country without influence, the media ignored them. For most of this decade the liberals have reacted hysterically to the growing influence of the New Right—much as they did to the anti-Communist movement of the 1960s.

Many of today's political leaders of the New Right were influenced directly or indirectly by Bill Buckley's Young Americans for Freedom. Another influential group was the American Conservative Union. Both of these organizations inspired activity on the college campuses of the nation, and as their disciples matured, many started their own conservative action groups.

The Heritage Foundation, established in 1973 by Paul Weyrich and Dr. Ed Fuelner with a generous grant from long-time conservative patriot Joe Coors, has supplied the research, credibility, and motivation to many of the New Right organizations, which have contributed to the re-educating of the American people. Two years later, Weyrich placed the leadership of Heritage in the capable hands of Ed Fuelner so that Paul could establish other political action groups. To show the effectiveness of the Heritage Foundation, we need only to look at its phenomenal growth. Since its small beginning (incorporated in January of 1974), it has become one of the "big four" think tanks in Washington, D.C., with a budget exceeding $11 million in 1985.

Other effective New Right organizations include Paul Weyrich's Committee for the Survival of a Free Congress (CSFC), founded in 1974 with financial help from Joe Coors. If I were to pick the most effective New Right leader today from a list which includes Howard Phillips, Richard Viguerie, Terry Dolan, Morton Blackwell, Dr. Ed Fuelner, Phyllis Schlafly, Reed Larson, and other gifted conservative patriots, I would select Paul Weyrich. Equipped with a razor-sharp mind, he is a master strategist, analyst, organizer, and coalition builder with two obsessions: to serve God as a man and father and to lead America back to traditional values and conservative principles. He has informed people how to win elections and has strategized the elections of key members of Congress. If he is as successful in the next decade as he has been in the last, America will enjoy a conservative Congress by the year 2000.

Mention must be made of Howard Phillips's very effective Conservative Caucus. A gifted tactician, Howard keeps a running tab on congressional voting patterns and is literally turning election day into judgment day for the liberal politicians who used to go to Washington and vote their liberal convictions, then return home and win elections by talking like conservatives. Howard has made it all but impossible for liberals to hide behind their voting records. In addition, he has developed a healthy strategy he calls "defunding the left," which focuses attention on the fact that left-wing organizations have been draining the federal till of tax dollars for decades.

I am convinced that if federal funding were cut off, Planned Parenthood, NOW, and many other left-wing organizations would go out of business in six months.

Terry Dolan's National Conservative Political Action Committee (NCPAC) has probably angered more liberals in and out of politics than any other group. He pioneered the independent expenditure program, which allows him to spend an unlimited amount of money on an election campaign—so long as he and the candidate are not in contact. In the two banner years of 1978 and 1980 NCPAC and other conservative organizations used the giveaway of the Panama Canal to rid the Senate of many liberal members by revealing their votes to their constituencies. Today liberals like George McGovern, Frank Church, Birch Bayh, and others are in private life where their liberalism should have less effect on the future of America.

Conservative activism during the next decade will not be as easy as in the past, largely because the left is aware of the New Right's existence. But more special interest groups are emerging, using New Right techniques to reach additional voters at a time when liberalism is floundering, backpedaling, and being exposed as an un-American fraud. As we shall see, we have reached a precarious point in history when the political control of this nation could pass into conservative hands or revert to liberal domination, either of which will have a powerful impact on the 21st century. If liberals return to total power in future elections, I am convinced they will take us to the United States of Sodom and Gomorrah. But if the present conservative trends continue, we will return to traditional moral values.

Direct Mail and the Religious Right

From a primitive beginning, direct mail has become a sophisticated computerized business that can enable a congressman or preacher to communicate personally two or three times a month with millions of supporters. It not only allows conservative candidates to raise the necessary millions of dollars they will need to get elected but also permits conservative leaders to educate millions of people in the process.

Richard Viguerie may not be the father of direct mail, but he is certainly the best known conservative in the field. Recognizing that the oil of politics is money, he inaugurated a direct mail company for conservative candidates. He does not help liberals (in fact, he has the distinction of refusing George McGovern as a client). He supports only those whom he believes will contribute to the conservative change our nation has needed these past fifty years.

One requirement Richard insists on before he accepts a client is ownership of the names that come in through that individual's campaign. Consequently, by representing many candidates, he has accumulated a massive number of names, perhaps the largest list of conservatives of anyone in the United States today (estimated at 30 million).

Many citizens call bulk mail "junk mail." In recent years I have gained a different perspective—and my mailbox is as full as yours. In fact, I seem to be on everybody's list! Admittedly, two or three mailings a week from the same ministry or political organization are excessive, but consider the process in a positive light.

1. It raises money for good candidates or causes (and if you don't like a person or cause, you can easily discard the appeal). In many cases this is the *only* way an organization can raise sufficient funds to unseat an entrenched incumbent who has access to incredible amounts of special-interest money from unions, NEA, liberal political action committees, and corporations.

2. Even more importantly, it educates millions of Americans weekly who would otherwise be uninformed about the truth of a particular issue.

Liberals and Direct Mail?

We may well ask, Can liberals catch up with the New Right in attracting financing for political campaigns through direct mail? And if so, how long will it take? Richard Viguerie says that the liberal establishment is about ten years behind conservatives but will someday pull even with them. Personally, I am not so sure that the left will ever be able to use the mail as effectively as the New Right. Three facts make this unlikely:

1. The left is largely made up of takers, not givers. One may be able to attract votes from welfare recipients and other special interest groups by offering them more federal money, but they will not give to help elect candidates. They are more interested in what politicians can do for them.

2. The philosophy of liberalism is selfish. Conservatives give well because we are taught that giving is a virtue. Liberals are part of the "me generation." Many of them want all the gusto they can get now because they believe, "When you're dead, you're dead." So why should they give? Besides, they expect the government to open wide its social coffers on a regular basis. When Teddy Kennedy appealed to Californians to raise money for Jerry Brown's Senate bid, he failed.

3. Liberals are still in control. Concerned conservatives will give by the millions to reverse five decades of liberalism. The motivation to retain control is not as powerful as the drive to gain control.

As I wrote the above lines, I received a letter from Pat Robertson. It included a six-page fund-raising letter written by Paul G. Kirk, Jr., chairman of the Democratic National Committee, using Pat's expected candidacy for president as a fear technique to enlist liberals to send him money by direct mail. I was all set to add one qualification to my third fact: liberals can only succeed with direct mail if they instigate a fear campaign among their followers. Kirk has done exactly that!

He calls Robertson "one of the most powerful public figures in America today" and "ultrafundamentalist" and several times identifies him as a member of the "religious right-wing." If that kind of inflammatory rhetoric doesn't inspire cold, naked fear in the liberal heart, nothing will. The prospect of a conservative Christian occupying the White House—and attacking abortion on demand, pornography, and free access to drugs—or urging a strong national defense, the extension of religious freedom for all, and criminal accountability—is enough to terrify even the most complacent liberal.

The Washington Post reported that only 500 responses to the Kirk letter were received out of the 50,000 mailed (and probably all of them did not send money). That is less than a 1 percent response, making it impossible for them to continue the mailing at this time. The reason? Liberals are takers—not givers!

Ronald Reagan—the Most Influential Conservative

If I were to select one person who has contributed most to the growing conservative revival in America during the past two decades, it would have to be Ronald Reagan. He has put his conservative theories to the test in the largest state in the union, leaving it after eight years with a financial surplus and a booming economy.

He has also given more speeches to a greater number of people than any other person during that period. His speeches reflect a consistent pattern of practical conservative doctrine, which emphasizes moral values, hard work, self-discipline, hope, opportunity, patriotism, and other conservative ideology. He has educated millions of people to become conservatives (by clarifying their basic

On July 9, 1984, Dr. LaHaye introduced President Reagan to 250 pastors who serve as congressional district chairman of the American Coalition for Traditional Values (a coalition of Bible-believing pastors interested in getting millions of Christians more involved in the political process).

yearnings) and has made conservatism respectable in spite of hostile media attempts to make him and his ideals look childish. Today even the skeptical Europeans acknowledge this former actor as a strong and persuasive leader.

But he is more than that; he is a teacher. He has turned America from the defeatist malaise of the Carter years (the natural result of liberalism) to an unbounded spirit of optimism toward the future. The American people are no longer afraid of tomorrow. They are excitedly anticipating the future as the time to harness the unlimited treasures of the sea and outer space. The commercial potentials of space are mind-boggling—potentials that will provide jobs and challenges for our children's children long after we have entered the 21st century.

In his inaugural address President Reagan reminded us that as a

A 1985 conference at the White House was called by the president to determine what his administration could do to help the families of the nation. Dr. James Dobson and Dr. LaHaye represented two evangelical organizations. Others were from religious and secular family life or support groups.

people we "are too great a nation to limit ourselves to small dreams." This spirit of conservative enthusiasm is sweeping the nation. Even many brainwashed victims of our left-leaning public system of education are heeding his conservative ideology. President Reagan will bequeath a conservative legacy to America long after he leaves public office, not only because he will have appointed more judges than any president in history, but because of his quarter of a century of preaching conservative doctrine—and his opportunity to show that it works. President Ronald Reagan will go down in history as one of our nation's top three presidents and certainly the most important in the twentieth century.

How Long Will It Last?

Will the current Conservative Megatrend last into the 21st century? Only God knows! I have good reason to believe it will, but no one is able to predict the future. For example, if we were suddenly plunged into a 1930-style depression, everything would change. The American people would probably look to government handouts to solve the problem and vote more liberal politicians back into office (even though the government itself with a $2 trillion deficit is near bankruptcy).

Barring such a national catastrophe in the next decade, it seems likely that the conservative movement has not yet reached its peak. Its roots seem solid and deep in the soil of college campuses, where new conservative newspapers and organizations are appearing regularly (much to the consternation of liberal professors, who formerly advocated "free speech" but now are hesitant to include conservatives).

Most of the conservative groups of the past two decades were launched as special interest groups, but as they matured they branched into other related fields and continued to influence an enormous number of people. Because these people are still "outsiders"—not accepted by the liberal elite—they still tend to work well together.

Under the direction of Paul Weyrich, a master at coalition building, such groups as Library Court, The Kingston Group, and others will provide these conservative leaders with an opportunity to work and plan together for common goals. Fifteen years ago that was unheard of, but conservative coalitions have proved that there is strength in union. Together they halted the harmful ERA, slowed the welfare state, fought further intrusion by government into families and churches, and are bringing to the nation a much-needed breath of freedom and respect for traditional moral and family values. And all of these contributions are striking a positive chord in the hearts of millions of Americans.

1988—the Indicator

Everyone knows that Ronald Reagan cannot succeed himself. Thus the election of 1988 will give liberals one more opportunity to enter the political battle arena without having to face a charismatic personality who is able to reach the hearts of people despite media criticism. If the Republicans send a truly conservative candidate into battle and the Democrats offer the typical liberal of the past fifty years, it will be a classic liberal/conservative shoot-out that will further educate the nation's voters.

But more is involved than just the White House. Liberals still dominate the Senate and exercise a stifling control over the House of Representatives. That can easily be seen by the votes on two issues: the prayer amendment, which garnered only 36 votes out of 100 in the Senate; and the president's first request for $100 million to aid the Contra Freedom Fighters of Nicaragua, which was voted down by 222 liberals in the House. Even though he later got the aid he requested by a change of 13 votes, those first votes, in my opinion, reflected the true ideology of those respective bodies. In spite of the fact that Russia has supplied $500 million in weapons to the Sandanistas, many of our representatives still have a difficult time understanding that the turmoil in Central America is caused by communism's policy of worldwide conquest.

What Check-and-Balance System?

To develop and maintain a truly conservative government, we must win a series of elections and add certain Supreme Court appointments between now and the 21st century. A conservative president alone cannot do it. In fact, we are supposed to have a check-and-balance system in our country, with the Supreme Court independent of the Congress, which in turn is independent of the president. In practice it becomes a liberal-dominated Supreme Court (the result of past liberal presidential appointments) and an equally liberal House and Senate ganging up on a conservative president to stifle his policies. The Senate has fought or refused to confirm many conservative presidential appointments, which means that a liberal Senate has refused to let a president—elected by the largest popular vote in history—appoint people who share his political conservatism. That is not check-and-balance but circumvention of the will of the people. Several elections are necessary to rectify such an imbalance.

Why, you may be asking, is it possible for the American people to elect a conservative president and not a majority of other conservative officials? The answer lies in the media. Our liberal press is able to clothe liberal representatives and senators with conservative respectability. Candidate weaknesses are hidden or buried on page 79 of the daily newspaper. But the media lampoon and ridicule conservative candidates, who otherwise have difficulty getting their message out to the people on page one. Even the press cannot hide a president's values and ideals, since public debate brings both presidential candidates into our homes.

Conservative and New Right groups look forward to the day they will be able to inform every citizen of the voting record of his senator and representative on issues of special interest before casting his ballot. That kind of informed voting promises to keep the Conservative Megatrend moving into the 21st century. In *The Third Wave,* Alvin Toffler predicted greater involvement by grassroots citizens in the activities of government during the next century. I suspect that he is right. But I don't think he expected it would be so overwhelmingly conservative.

Can you imagine what America would be like if a majority of its elected government leaders shared the country's conservative values and if five of our Supreme Court justices were as conservative as our president? Government would initiate legislative reform that has been needed in this country for over a quarter of a century.

Pornographers wouldn't like it. Abortionists, feminists, secular humanists, and ACLU lawyers already wring their hands thinking about the possibility. But the majority of the American people could convey what Congressman Newt Gingrich calls the conservative "Opportunity Society" to their children.

Recommended Reading

Allen, Gary. *None Dare Call It Conspiracy.* Seal Beach, Cal.: Concord Press, n.d.

Chambers, Whittaker. *The Witness.* N.Y.: Random House, 1952.

Fox, Victor J. *The Pentagon Case.* N.Y.: Freedom Press, 1958.

Goldwater, Barry M. *Conscience of a Conservative.* N.Y.: Manor Books, 1974. (This may have been the most influential of them all, selling three million copies in hardback and millions more in paperback.)

Hoover, J. Edgar. *Masters of Deceit.* N.Y.: Holt, Rinehart, and Winston, 1958.

Philbrick, Herbert, *I Led Three Lives.* N.Y.: McGraw-Hill, 1952.

Russell, Kirk. *The Conservative Mind.* Lake Bluff, Ill.: Regnery-Gateway, n.d.

Schaeffer, Francis A. *How Should We Then Live?* Westchester, Ill.: Good News, 1983. (and other books by Dr. Schaeffer)

Schlafly, Phyllis. *A Choice Not an Echo.* Alton, Ill.: Pere Marquette, 1964.

Schwartz, Fred. *You Can Trust the Communists—To Be Communists.* Englewood Cliffs, N.J.: Prentice-Hall, 1960.

Skousen, W. Cleon. *The Naked Communist.* Salt Lake City: The Reviewer, 1962.

Stormer, John A. *Death of a Nation.* Orem, Utah: Liberty Bell Press, 1983.

———— *None Dare Call It Treason.* Orem, Utah: Liberty Bell Press, n.d.

———— 6 ————

The Merging of Two Giant Megatrends: The "New Right" and the "Religious Right"

The future of America is still undecided. Whether President Reagan has charted a new course that will set our compass for decades—or whether history will see him as the conservative interruption in a process of inexorable national decline—is yet to be determined. If the force and energy and dedication and yes, faith, that are in this room, can be multiplied many times over and focused upon this city, there is no force here that can stand up to it. Which is why I think that, in the end, not they but we shall overcome.

Patrick J. Buchanan, White House Communications Director speaking to the National Religious Broadcasters Convention Washington, D.C., February 1986

O N January 22, 1980, President Jimmy Carter made what I consider to be a monumental mistake. Without realizing the historic results of his action, President Carter invited twelve Christian leaders to breakfast at the White House: Dr. Jerry Falwell, Dr. D. James Kennedy, Dr. Charles Stanley, Jim Bakker, Rex Humbard, Oral Roberts, a representative of the Billy Graham organization, me, and several others. This meeting will not be recorded as a turning point in American history, but it helped to convince these members of the Born-again Megatrend that they must increase their efforts to influence the political decisions of our country.

In order to understand the significance of this event, we must go back in history to what I call the fundamentalist fallacy of the past fifty years.

The Fallacy of Nonparticipation

Most of today's Christian leaders were reared under the false teaching that Christians should not be involved in the political process. As my godly pastor used to say, "Politics is a dirty business! We Christians should never get involved in politics. We should spend our lives advancing the Kingdom of God and leave the politics to the nice, civic-minded people."

Fifty years later Christians are waking up to discover that "the nice, civic-minded people," who have filled the government vacuum created by such reasoning, have turned out to be not so nice and even less civic. They have changed our Judeo-Christian country, which proudly proclaimed itself "one nation under God," into a libertine society, "a secular nation."

A Secular Nation?

Unfortunately many Christians in this country have been convinced by secular humanists in education and members of the American Civil Liberties Union (ACLU) that the American government should be religiously neutral or secular. Many of us studied the "separation of church and state" in civics or American government. Those words, which do not appear in the U.S. Constitution, have been misinterpreted to mean that government should be protected from religion; however, our founders meant to protect religion from government interference. After all, the Pilgrims and others came to America to escape religious persecution.

Our forefathers balanced the secular and the religious by keeping the state out of the church and by refusing to let the state become "sectarian" by adopting a state religion. The First Amendment prohibits government from establishing a state church as was done in England, Germany, and the state of Virginia. It does not keep members of the church (or even ministers) from participating in government or politics!

Most of us did not realize what this false teaching would do to our country's government. There can be no such thing as secular neutrality. True religion is so all-encompassing that it influences everything in our lives. To truly secularize the state, one must exclude religion. A proposed neutrality becomes hostility. In a secular state, for instance, a judge must not let his religious values influence his decisions. That is not only impossible if he is deeply religious but morally dangerous. Is that what our founding fathers wanted? I think not.

Not only was secularism changing the great separation of government and church issue into a separation-of-government-from-God policy, but most evangelicals felt betrayed by Jimmy Carter. When Carter ran against Gerald Ford in 1976, most Bible-believing ministers were either silenced by his well-advertised claim to be a born-again Southern Baptist deacon and Sunday school teacher or actively worked to register the members of their congregations and get them to the polls on election day so they could vote for him. It is estimated that over 2 million Christians left the Republican party that year to vote for one of their own. Some believe that the born-again issue made Jimmy Carter our thirty-ninth president.

Four years later Christian leaders were still waiting for Jimmy Carter to introduce the ideas and programs they had expected him to favor. Oh, he taught Sunday school on Sunday when he could, but as president he largely ignored us in his appointments. His political agenda was also different from ours: he favored the Equal Rights Amendment, refused to promote anti-abortion legislation or even halt government-funded abortions, opposed a School Prayer Amendment, and appointed more liberal judges than any president in American history. In short, he campaigned as a Christian conservative but ran his administration as a Christian liberal. When he began running for re-election, he decided to rebuild a bridge to the people who helped to elect him the first time.

The Historic Meeting

Jimmy Carter invited those conservative Christian leaders I mentioned at the beginning of this chapter to a special breakfast so we could ask him seven questions that troubled us (as long as we submitted them in writing in advance). Dr. Jerry Falwell broke the ice that morning by asking President Carter why he opposed the abortion amendment; Dr. Kennedy inquired why in the face of godless

The January 22, 1980, breakfast meeting with President Jimmy Carter and several Christian leaders, convinced many of us that his liberal policies were harmful to the families and future of America.

Communists' military build-up he rejected a strong national defense; I wanted to know why he favored the Equal Rights Amendment in view of the harmful effects it would have on the nation's families. The president was obviously ill at ease with these questions, and in my opinion, his answers were inadequate.

Finally, Morris Sheets, a Dallas pastor who admittedly was one of Carter's supporters in 1976, asked a question that destroyed any of the false congeniality that remained. "Why, Mr. President, have you not appointed one single known Christian to your cabinet or other visible position of influence in your administration?"

I well remember his answer. Clearing his throat, he responded, "I don't think that is a fair appraisal of my administration. I have brought several religious people into my government. I brought Vice President Walter Mondale into my administration, and he is a very religious man; his father was a minister. I also brought Ann

Wexler, Secretary of Agriculture Berglund, and, of course, I brought Rosalyn into my government."

His answer was inadequate, since according to his own words, Walter Mondale is a humanist, and Ann Wexler, who served as Carter's public relations person and had set up our breakfast meeting, is a Jewess.

After that meeting, I stood by the wrought-iron gates of the White House with five of the other men, waiting for our car. I bowed my head and prayed, *Oh, God, we must get this man out of the White House. America cannot survive another four years of his administration.* The five of us got into the car and rode in silence to our destinations. My spirit of depression seemed to be shared by all.

That group of ministers never called a strategy meeting, but most of us left determined to use whatever influence we had to make sure that Christians knew Jimmy Carter's political philosophy before they voted for him again. I returned to the three churches I pastored at the time and preached a message on the policies of the Carter

Dr. LaHaye asked President Carter why he was promoting the Equal Rights Amendment in view of the fact that it would prove so harmful to family life in America.

administration. I then distributed cassette tapes of the sermon to ministers around the country; many copied the tapes and spread them even further. One businessman supplied tapes of my sermon to 10,000 of his employees. Later that year my congregation in San Diego joined my wife and me in financing the free mailing of my first book exposing secular humanism, *The Battle for the Mind*, to 85,000 ministers in America. We asked them to read it and teach its concepts to their people.

The sleeping giant of the Christian church was beginning to awaken to the importance of politics, and some Christians were ready to join hands with others in the nation who were eager for a return to traditional values.

The Coalition of Merging Megatrends

Conservative Paul Weyrich is often accused by the liberals of inspiring Dr. Jerry Falwell with the idea for the Moral Majority. Actually it was an idea whose time had come. The Religious Right, a term used to describe the Protestant fundamentalists of the Born-again Megatrend, was prepared to set aside some of its religious prejudices in order to work with other conservative Americans, not only to restore traditional values but to preserve the most important right of all—religious freedom.

The Religious Right began to merge with the New Right, or conservative megatrend, in 1979 and 1980. Although members of these two groups may reflect divergent theological views and different religious loyalties, they share so many mutual social concerns that they are increasingly found fighting together for the preservation of our nation's moral heritage.

The 1973 *Roe vs. Wade* decision to legalize abortion has probably done more than anything else to bring about a merging of political activities between conservatives and religious fundamentalists. Add to that a mutual concern for our weakened laws against pornography, runaway crime, and rape, and you have ample reason why these two megatrends have coalesced into an effective force against liberal humanism, a coalition that would have seemed impossible just a decade ago.

The Religious Right and the New Right carry on simultaneous activities based on their basic conservative philosophy and often merge in their voting patterns to form a political coalition. However, they will never merge as organizations. Each has its own base constituency to educate and activate, and—let's face it—each is directed by strong individualists. By working simultaneously for the same concerns, however, they can supplement and reinforce each other's objectives. I have yet to meet a conservative who wants to secularize America.

In the early days, Paul Weyrich and Howard Phillips were invaluable teachers of the political process to many of the religious leaders who were often politically naive. Most of us were preachers who had never been involved in politics and had, in fact, believed that ministers should stay out of politics.

In 1978 I called a group of California ministers together and organized Californians for Biblical Morality—my first attempt to halt the secularizing of my state. In 1979 Jerry Falwell, who usually thinks fifty times bigger than I do, invited Dr. Greg Dixon of Indianapolis and me to join him as incorporating board members of the Moral Majority, which he intended to establish in all fifty states. He later added Dr. Kennedy, Dr. Stanley, and others to the board, reflecting Christian leaders' growing concern that government was transforming America into a secular and immoral society and that the Christian policy of noninvolvement must be abandoned. In addition, the Religious Roundtable, organized by Ed McAteer; the Christian Voice, founded by Colonel Doner; and many other Christian political groups were instituted, showing the simultaneous concern of Christians for the sick state of the Union.

In recent years the Moral Majority (now known as the Liberty Federation) has grown to over 4 million members; the organization provides a hard-hitting monthly newspaper on the issues and raises close to $12 million annually to educate Christians on the moral/governmental issues of our day. Concerned Women for America, led by my wife Beverly, was actually founded in 1978 before the Moral Majority. It has grown to almost 600,000 members, making it, according to *Time* magazine, "larger than NOW, the Women's Political Caucus and the League of Women Voters combined."[1]

In 1984 I invited most of the nation's leading media evangelists to join me in establishing the American Coalition for Traditional Values (ACTV), the broadest coalition of Bible-believing ministers ever assembled. Putting aside our theological differences, we built a Washington, D.C.-based organization on our mutual moral concerns for this nation. During that year, together with others, we registered an additional 2 million Christian voters and educated millions on the positions of the presidential and congressional candidates. We have built a network to most of the 435 congressional districts by selecting a chairman pastor to transmit camera-ready educational materials to all pastors in his district. Within ten days to two weeks we can reach millions of Christians in this country and encourage them to voice their opinions on a moral issue to our federal leaders.

Unfortunately, we do not yet have the votes in either the Senate or House to implement our moral concerns, so we are now encouraging Christians to run for public office or to become campaign volunteers for candidates who share their values. If through ACTV or any other similar organization we can train 300 to 500 Christians per congressional district to campaign for congressional candidates who share their moral values, we will see a marked change in the philosophy of the Congress in the next decade. A reformation in Washington will eventually reflect itself in society at large.

There are more than enough Christians in this country to halt the secular takeover of our society. A CBS-*New York Times* exit poll during the 1984 election found that 12 million voters were born again, 80 percent of whom voted for conservative Ronald Reagan.[2] Bear in mind, Jack Kennedy was elected in 1960 by only 500,000 votes. Christian political involvement in the future *can* make the difference!

But Is It Scriptural?

A well-known Bible teacher announced, "I disapprove of today's preachers who are encouraging Christians to become politically active. Jesus did not urge His disciples to overthrow the Roman government."

Because this thinking is shared by many faithful pastors, it would be well for me to provide an extended answer.

What Does the Bible Say?

In Matthew 5, our Lord said, "You are the salt of the earth" and "the light of the world" (vv. 13, 14). Many ministers fail to realize that during the past fifty years we have done a good job of being the light of the world, but a very poor job of acting as the salt of the earth.

According to Gallup, Christianity has tripled in the last fifty years—but our culture is much worse morally than when we had fewer Christians. Why? Because Christians have withdrawn from government, an institution established by God Himself. Consequently, secularists who are either neutral toward religion and its values or hostile toward them have become our nation's leaders.

Christians represent "4 out of 10" people in our country, according to Gallup,[3] but only 10 to 15 percent of our elected officials represent a Christian commitment. Our numbers greatly exceed our influence. Yet three times in Romans 13:1–6, God calls government authorities "ministers of God . . . for good" (kjv).

Do pastors have a biblical responsibility to encourage their parishioners to fulfill God's description of our leaders? I think so. The Old Testament alludes to many government leaders as "ministers of God": Moses, Samuel, King David, King Solomon, Daniel, Isaiah, Gideon. It is unscriptural to proclaim that government is not the Christian's business (see Rom. 13:1–6; 1 Tim. 2:1–5).

I believe that pastors should also expose leaders who are not "ministers of God for good." In Ephesians 5:10–14 we are taught that it is acceptable to God to expose the unfruitful workers of darkness. Judges who approve abortions on demand and are soft on criminals and pornographers should be called to account for their actions and replaced on election day by those who share the moral values of our founding fathers. Unfortunately the faithful pastor who hastens to identify a theological heretic to his congregation is often mute when it comes to pointing a finger at elected officials whose philosophies cause them to vote in favor of anti-moral legislation.

In the early years of our country, God used Christians to create a social and moral environment that was conducive to the spread of the gospel. The more salt we supply to our generation by becoming involved in the political process, the better our light will shine to the lost souls in the country.

Today's Moral Activists

If my voice were the only one being raised to awaken the sleeping church of Jesus Christ to its moral responsibility, I would fear that I was not being led by the Holy Spirit. But that is not the case. Some of the best-known pastors and preachers in the nation are diligently promoting the involvement of Christians in the political arena. Most of these men are active in ACTV. Consider some of these men of God. . . .

Dr. Jerry Falwell, the most outspoken of our group, has only been a Christian thirty years, yet he pastors one of the largest churches in the nation. Seen on television each week in more than 300 cities, he has founded a Christian college with over 5,000 students and envisions the day he will have an enrollment of 50,000. He is asking God to let him be the inspiration for starting over 5,000 new churches.

Dr. Jimmy Swaggart is the second most watched television evangelist of our day. The Nielsen ratings claim that 9 million families watch his program regularly,[4] and his crusades attract some of the largest crowds in the country. He has launched a Bible college, pastors a booming church, and gives over $10 million a year to missionary causes around the world. Yet he raises his voice in opposition to the liberal policies of secular humanists in government and is actively engaged in urging Christians either to run for public office or to campaign for those candidates who share their moral values.

Dr. D. James Kennedy, pastor of the largest Presbyterian church in the nation, is seen on over 175 TV stations weekly. Through his Evangelism Explosion International he has trained more church people in the art of personal soul winning than any pastor in the country. Yet his scholarly voice is dedicated to exposing secular humanism as the number one cause of the breakdown in moral values. At a recent ACTV conference he said, "Five of my members have already filed to run for public office, and I believe that number will reach twelve by the '86 elections. It is my prayer that fifty of my people will run by 1988."

Dr. James Dobson, psychologist and president of Focus on the Family, has ministered to millions through his films, books, and radio ministry, which is heard thirty minutes daily on over 1,000 stations. Although he never supports or opposes political candidates, he does regularly inform his listeners concerning moral issues and urges them to action. As a result of one broadcast, his listeners sent more than 100,000 letters in support of regulations to protect handicapped babies. On other occasions he motivated the writing of hundreds of thousands of letters sent to Washington in favor of prayer in schools, tax reduction for families, anti-pornography efforts, and regulations making it illegal for organizations to lobby Congress with money obtained from the government. "We do not issue this kind of request for support very often," he said. "But our listeners are extremely responsive in those instances where public reaction has been needed."

Dr. Pat Robertson, the host of the most popular Christian television program, "The 700 Club," according to a recent Nielsen rating,[5] is viewed in 17 million homes. He directs a $230-million-a-year communications ministry and has given millions of dollars to hundreds of mission projects in this country and abroad. He has exposed the evils of secular humanism many times on his program and on Christian Broadcasting Network (CBN), his cable TV network, which goes into 34 million homes. Robertson estimates that over 1 million souls have come to faith through his television ministry.

Pat has founded the Freedom Council to encourage Christians to become politically active. He has also instituted a Christian law school for the purpose of raising up a new generation of lawyers, judges, and politicians. His concern for government is so strong that he is praying about running for president of the United States in 1988!

The Southern Baptist denomination is not without its very concerned pastors. Three of the past presidents are founders of ACTV and are aggressive in many moral, political, and religious freedom issues. Many of our congressional district chairmen are Southern Baptist pastors.

Dr. Charles Stanley, former president of the Southern Baptist Convention and pastor of the growing First Baptist Church of Atlanta, Georgia, telecasts his church service to over 200 cities and speaks out for Christian involvement in the governmental process. So does *Dr. Jimmy Draper,* pastor of the eleven-year-old First Baptist Church of Euless, Texas, where he speaks each Sunday to over 5,000 people. *Dr. Adrian Rogers,* re-elected president of the Southern Baptist Convention in 1986, is one of the outstanding soul-winning pastors in the nation.

All three of these soul-winning pastors helped to found ACTV, and they regularly call Christians to get involved.

Dr. Bill Bright, founder and president of Campus Crusade for Christ International, is not only a personal soul winner but has probably taught more Christians how to share their faith than anyone since the apostle Paul. His program numbers 16,000 staff members worldwide, representing a great burden for lost souls both in America and abroad, yet he, too, urges Christians to become involved in politics.

Rev. Bob Tilton ministers to 3,000 souls in Dallas each week; by video satellite he transmits his services, including seminars on secular humanism and the necessity of political involvement, to over 1,800 churches.

Some of the other concerned ministers are my pastor, *Dr. Bill Weber,* of Prestonwood Baptist Church (often called the fastest-growing church in the history of Southern Baptists); *Pastor Ed Young,* who mobilized 350 pastors to vote down the "gay rights" legislation sponsored by the liberal Houston city council; and pastors of some of the largest churches in the nation, like *Marvin Rickard,* of Los Gatos, California, and *John Gimenez,* an ACTV board member whose Rock Church in Virginia Beach has over 10,000 in attendance. John also organized the "Washington for Jesus" march that brought 500,000 Christians to the nation's capital. The list must include *Tommy Barnett* in Phoenix, *Dr. Ed Nelson* and *Charles Blair* in Denver, *Don George* in Dallas, and *Truman Dollar* in Detroit. Sometimes politically active pastors are accused of "giving up preaching and soul winning for politics." But as the above list indicates, just the opposite is true, for they are among the leading soul winners in the nation.

The timely concern of these godly men and thousands of pastors like them tells us that God the Holy Spirit is moving on the hearts of his church and its leaders to become the savoring influence our Lord commanded us to be. During the next decade an enormous number of Christians will be running for public office, and some 50,000 to 100,000 Christians will begin working on behalf of those who share their values. Millions of unregistered believers will register and go to the polls on election day as faithful citizens.

The humanists' goal is for America to become a humanist nation by the year 2000. The one group they do not control is the evangelical church of Jesus Christ. By awakening Christians to their civic responsibility, we can lead this nation back to moral decency through the election of a new breed of legislator: one who believes that "righteousness exalts a nation," that civil morality is good for America.

But Is It Legal?

Many Christians may be intimidated into silence on politics because they fear that somehow their church might lose its tax-exempt status. So far none of us who have taken an aggressive stand on these issues has done anything to cause our tax-exempt status to be revoked. Ministers are only forbidden to endorse candidates in the pulpit or raise money in church for them—neither of which we would do anyway. The truth is, Christians have far more legal privileges than we realize.

As private individuals, ministers are able to support candidates as well as recruit, train, and educate their members on the issues and the positions of the candidates. Many of us believe that ministers have a moral obligation to do so but not as part of the worship service; therefore, some ministers pass out educational materials as their members exit the church. Others send it by direct mail; still others have the handouts put on car windshields in the parking lots.[6]

Some members of the Religious Right get impatient with the still-sleeping Christians who either fail to recognize or refuse to engage in our struggle for the survival of traditional values. But I am encouraged.

Each year more ministers join the movement. Some are awakened to the issues when their church's application for a building permit is rejected by a liberal city council or when a school board in their community demands explicit sex education classes for children. Others see the light when pornography destroys a family in their church. For many it is the relentless cry of the 4,000 fetuses a day who are legally murdered by abortion.

Every election more get involved. I expect that another 3 million Christians will be registered during the elections of 1986 and 1988, and thousands of others will either run for public office or campaign in behalf of those who share their moral values.

In the last decade more evangelical Christians have become involved politically than at any time since before the Revolutionary War or the Civil War. Concerned Catholics, Jews, and other religious citizens are becoming involved also, all seeking elected officials deeply committed to traditional moral values.

The New Sectarian Cooperation

Unfortunately, during the first half of the twentieth century, Protestants fought so much among themselves and against Roman Catholics over doctrinal differences that they could not even cooperate politically. In fact, Catholics founded their own parochial schools to "keep our children," their prelates declared, "out of those Protestant public schools." Having inherited a Christian consensus society, various religions enjoyed the luxury of struggling over doctrinal purity, while paying little attention to society's declining moral standards.

Gradually the religiously minded people began to notice a change in our Judeo-Christian society. I remember hearing the cries of the Catholic pro-life leaders after the *Roe vs. Wade* decision in 1973 and feeling that their stand—"The mass of tissue in a woman's womb is a living human being"—was, in fact, God's truth. But like many Protestant ministers, I did little about it until 1976.

Now, almost fifteen years and over 18 million abortions later, we are experiencing a growing respect for some of these other religious Americans with whom we share moral concerns. That respect does not lessen our theological differences, but it does make us realize that one denomination does not have a corner on moral concerns for our culture. In fact, Catholics, Protestants, Jews, and others are developing a common concern that secularizers would, if they could, destroy the religious freedoms of us all.

Thirty years ago many of us subconsciously (or perhaps even consciously) felt that religious freedom really pertained only to our religion. But we were forced to reconsider our narrow interpretation when secularizers and atheists extended their interpretation of the First Amendment and other laws in this country (such as zoning laws)—first, to restrict cults from passing out literature in public places and then, to keep Christians from holding Bible studies in their homes (as the mayor of Los Angeles did in September of 1980); and finally, to exclude the Ten Commandments, Easter and Christmas holidays, and the Christmas creche from our public schools and our town halls. We are beginning to realize that if we do not stand together as religious groups, we will gradually lose our individual religious freedoms to those who look on all religion as unnecessary and potentially harmful.

One religious group by itself cannot save this country from a secular takeover. Born-again Christians are the largest minority in the nation, but at best we represent only 40 percent of the population. The Catholics cannot do it alone, because they comprise approximately 20 percent. But working together as fellow citizens on a basis of mutual moral concerns, we could exercise a powerful influence to preserve religious liberty and moral sanity for all.

Liberals love to see us fight among ourselves. Once when I appeared on a Phil Donahue show, Phil tried to insert a religious question into a debate on secular humanism.

"Do you mean to say that if a Jew does not accept Jesus Christ as his Lord and Savior, he will go to hell?" he asked me.

That inflammatory question could start a religious war on any corner of our country, and Phil Donahue realized it. He knew that I believe in our Lord's proclamation, "I am the way, the truth, and the life. No one comes to the Father except through Me" (John 14:6). Interestingly enough, that question has nothing to do with religious freedom or civil moral values.

However, Protestants, Catholics, and Jews do share two very basic beliefs:

- We all believe in God to Whom we must give account some day for the way we live our lives.
- We share a basic concern for the moral values that are found in the Old Testament.

If religious Americans work together in the name of our mutually shared moral concerns, we just might succeed in re-establishing the civic moral standards that our forefathers thought were guaranteed by the Constitution.

Is That Theological Compromise?

I realize that such statements may cause me to lose my fundamentalist membership card, but I really believe that we are in a fierce battle for the very survival of our culture, which we have been losing until recently because the other side has been the only one fighting.

Obviously, I am not suggesting joint evangelistic crusades with these religions; that would reflect an unacceptable theological compromise for all of us. But if we wish to maintain the right to share our faith door-to-door, send tracts and books through the mail, or rent television time to evangelize others, we must be willing to work for the preservation of everyone's right to do so.

All of our nation's religious citizens need to develop a respect for other religious people and their beliefs. We need not accept their beliefs, but we can respect the people and realize that we have more in common with each other than we ever will with the secularizers of this country. It is time for all religiously committed citizens to unite against our common enemy.

Polarizing the Nation

This ideological battle between religious and secular citizens is currently tearing our country apart, just as the Civil War did. One question is at the center of this conflict: Is America a secular nation that has no room for God and His moral absolutes in its public policy? Or is it a religious nation based on biblical principles?

I already told you my reasons for believing that our nation is, in fact, a "nation under God." Now let's look at the words of some of the founders of our country.

In his farewell address of 1796, our first president said:

Of all the dispositions and habits which lead to a political prosperity, religion and morality are indispensable supports. In vain would that man claim to tribute of patriotism, who should labour to subvert these great pillars of human happiness. . . .[7]

John Adams, our second president, recognized the need for religious and moral values:

We have no government armed in power capable of contending in human passions unbridled by morality and religion. Our Constitution was made only for a moral and religious people. It is wholly inadequate for the government of any other.[8]

The founders of this country actually called for the accommodation of religion—all religions—by the state. Political authority must not be hostile to religion or endorse one sect or denomination above another; it must assure the freedom of religion for all. We have obviously been led way off course in the secularizing of this great nation.

While it is understandable that in a free country some people in high places would favor a total secularization of our nation as beneficial for the future, it is improper for them to impose that philosophy on the nation at large for two reasons: (1) it is contrary to our Constitution and the intent of our founding fathers; and (2) they only represent a minority of the population, 10 to 20 percent at best.

Interestingly, the vast majority of the American people consider themselves religious. A 1984 Gallup Poll indicated that when Americans were asked to make a choice, 84 percent (including the unchurched) claimed "Christian" as their religion. If we add Jews and others, we approach a 94 percent religious majority, leaving only the 6 to 8 percent who claim atheism.

The results of the battle between religious and secular ideologies will probably be finalized during the 1990s in time to determine whose values will prevail in the 21st century. Each group can marshal an impressive array of followers, and each is vying for the votes on election day. Figures 1 and 2 explain my interpretation of the philosophical base and make-up of the two groups—and the people they would influence.

Figure 1

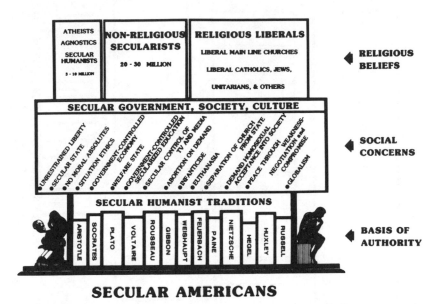

SECULAR AMERICANS

The base of this philosophy is man's wisdom, not God's. Although its policies during the past 50 years have caused many to become disenchanted with its conclusions, it maintains a firm grip on the thinking of many judges, lawyers, educators, journalists, media leaders, legislators, government employees, and others in influential positions.

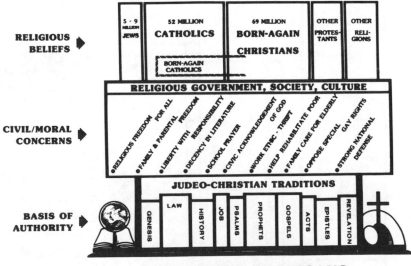

RELIGIOUS AMERICANS

The base of this philosophy is divine revelation, held to one degree or another by most religious leaders and people. Even many nonchurched Americans identify with this basic philosophy. A growing number of this persuasion are running for public office, serving as judges, lawyers, and educators, and seeking to work in the secular and religious media.

Figure 2

The Contrasting Philosophies of America

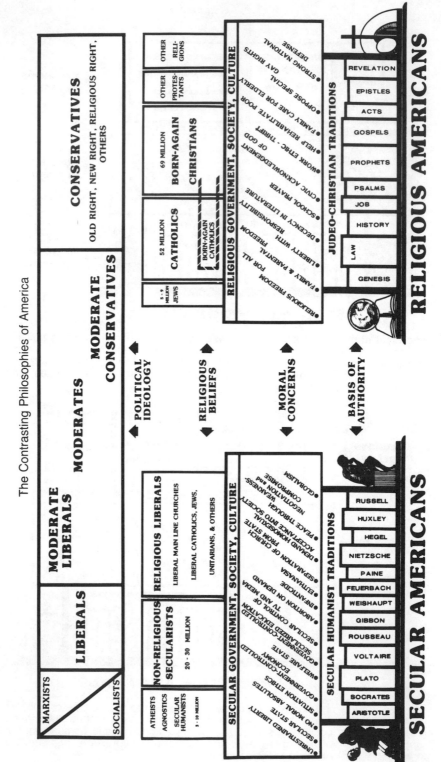

While analyzing the charts, we must remember that many influences affect the thinking of our 240 million citizens. Some religious people classify themselves as liberals; although they agree with our basic moral values individually, they have bought the liberal argument that such values should not be imposed on society legally. (That is why they personally oppose abortion and pornography but do not favor legislation to rectify these evils.) Generally, such individuals have either spent several years attending college and graduate school where they have been exposed to secular humanist thinking, or they live in a city with only one liberal newspaper. These people often fall prey to the media characterization of conservatives as "extremists," "fanatics," and "bigots."

The opposite is also true. Some conservatives are nonbelievers. They reject liberalism and have become active or moderate conservatives without realizing the basic biblical origins. Generally they are not hostile to religious conservatives, but they do not want to be pestered by attempts at evangelism either. Political conservatives and political liberals have been influenced to some degree by "the Christian consensus" (the Christian or religious influence of our founding fathers on our culture from the seventeenth century until the present).

Admittedly, the numbers on this chart are based on my personal observations as well as the Gallup and other polls and voting patterns. This estimate may be somewhat muddied by the plurality of the two major political parties since both Republicans and Democrats have some liberal and some conservative members. However, since Ronald Reagan appeared on the national scene in 1976, the Republican party has become more conservative; a few conservative Democrats have even shifted to the Republican party (such as Senator Phil Gramm, Jeanne Kirkpatrick, and Pat Robertson). Though the Democrats are aware of the growing conservative mood of the country and are trying to position themselves more toward the moderate or middle position, it is difficult for them to shake off the dominating control of their leaders, who may be personally religious but usually identify with a liberal church and separate their religious beliefs from their liberal political decisions.

Heretofore we have given little thought to the religious beliefs of our elected officials. Justice Sandra Day O'Connor was asked questions by the U.S. Senate before being confirmed as a Supreme Court justice, but no one inquired whether or not she believed in God. It seems that it is no longer a relevant question. Yet one's belief or disbelief in God will or should have a significant influence on every other life decision—and the life of the nation. That is extremely important if the person is a legislator.

I am not saying that America should become a Christian nation. I would be the first to oppose making Christianity a test for holding government office. By the same token, Christians, Jews, and other religious people ought not to be discriminated against because they are religious.

Some of the greatest criticism against me since I opened an office in Washington, D.C., was hurled by the *Washington Post* when I suggested that if we born-again Christians represent 25 to 30 percent of the population, we should hold 25 to 30 percent of the public offices in the land. The same should be true for all religious groups—Catholic, Protestant, Jewish. We all have the right to work for balanced representation in government.

Many tough moral decisions will confront our legislators in the nineties. The next century will best be served if those decisions are made by a representative number of politicians (regardless of party) who have their moral values deeply imbedded in religious values. As one American, I believe that the secularists have been in charge of our society for too long. They have already made too many harmful decisions that are destroying the moral fabric of our nation and its families.

It is time for a change! And gradually that change is coming.

STEP THREE

Determine Your Vision of the Future

7

What If Conservatives Gain Political Control?

If America is to survive, we must elect more God-centered men and women to public office; individuals who will seek divine guidance in the affairs of state. Christians should get involved in good government—not to conform, but to transform. . . . I would like to see every true believer involved in politics in some way, shape, or form.[1]

Dr. Billy Graham

LATE in 1985 I was invited to a conference at Wheaton, Illinois, attended by scholars, journalists, political science professors from Christian colleges, and other influential leaders. The discussion focused upon "Bible, politics, and democracy." I found the two-day conference particularly interesting in that representatives from the Religious Right seemed outnumbered by evangelical moderate conservatives and liberal moderates.

During the closing hour of that conference, someone finally asked the unspoken question that seemed to be on the minds of many people. "When you conservatives finally take control in America, what will you do?"

Frankly, I was disturbed that these Christian brothers were more afraid of Jerry Falwell and Pat Robertson than of Teddy Kennedy, Walter Mondale, and Justice William Powell. I had assumed that all Christians would be delighted to see our nation return to the traditional values of our founders. Evidently that is not true, particularly to those in the pursuit of their graduate degrees, overexposed to liberal thinkers.

Further reflection on these people's reactions convinced me that we conservatives have not adequately explained our vision for the future. We have been so busy trying to awaken the sleeping majority, both in and outside the church, that we have not really addressed the subject.

You Don't Have to Fear Conservatives

No one need fear conservative political influence. Why? First, this is a nation of law, and conservatives are committed to the preservation of the U.S. Constitution. Liberals are the ones who want to rewrite the Constitution or interpret its meaning differently from our founding fathers.

Second, the conservative movement is forced to battle a hostile press in seeking to gain the approval and votes of the people. Any violation of their conservative principles would appear on page one and be hammered out on the evening news. Our liberal media would make sure that an inconsistent conservative leadership would be short-lived.

Third, the conservative movement is made up of many diverse groups with differing loyalties and special interests, working voluntarily in union. The margin of victory at the polls is so slim that one group cannot afford to alienate any other faction. I have already noted that this coalition is made up of moderates, old right, New Right, Religious Right, secular conservatives, Catholics, Jews, Protestants, fundamentalists, and others. If one segment begins to dominate the conservative coalition and depart from the conservative political philosophy, the coalition will unravel and come to naught in future elections.

Conservative Dreams for America

If you want a short course in conservative dreams for America, just pay attention to the agenda of Ronald Reagan. Few want more for this country than he does—or have sacrificed more to get it. He could have retired to a well-deserved rest on his beloved ranch at seventy-four years of age. Instead, he plunged into another four years as president to finish what he had begun. Few Americans are afraid of Ronald Reagan's agenda.

In describing the conservative dreams for America, we must keep in mind that although there is basic agreement on the issues, we may find disagreement with regard to priorities. For example, secular conservatives may put a strong national defense first, while we fundamentalist ministers may elevate religious freedom or the protection of human life.

The following list is not intended to represent the conservative movement, for as far as I know, a summit conference has never hammered out such an agenda. This list, which reflects my own thinking, includes the ten moral concerns of the American Coalition for Traditional Values as well as a few other goals evangelicals see as important.

1. Establish religious freedom for all.

In the spirit of Roger Williams (the founder of Providence, Rhode Island, and a strong proponent of religious freedom for all) I believe this nation must protect every expression of religion and assure the equal right of all to communicate their faith. Government should not intrude into religion, except to protect human life in instances such as the human sacrifices of Satan worship or the enforcement of reasonable fire codes for church buildings.

If we truly believe our Lord's words, "And you shall know the truth, and the truth shall make you free" (John 8:32), we have nothing to fear in guaranteeing the equal opportunity for all religions to propagate their faith. What we should fear is a totalitarian secularist state that would expel religion from the media (particularly television and radio) as it has from education. While it is true that people are coming to Christ in Russia and China, converts would be multiplied many times if the Christian preachers there had equal access to the media, education, and other means of communication.

Government policy should never be used to promote any particular religion or sect, but neither should our leaders or policy prohibit the acknowledgment of a Supreme Being and His moral absolutes, even in our public schools. The humanists have convinced our courts that prayer represents the establishment of a religion. That is an atheistic view. Prayer is not religion but a universal expression of religion. Allowing prayer in our schools should not be prohibited in a free society nor should renting school property to community religious groups who can afford it. Our current policy favors atheism rather than freedom.

2. Pass a human life amendment to reverse _Roe vs. Wade_ and render illegal the immoral practice of abortion.

This would not only save millions of unborn babies but would also elevate respect for human life, protect the lives of unwanted or impaired infants (from infanticide), and safeguard the elderly (against euthanasia). We cannot give some government bureaucrats the power to decide who should or should not continue to live.

Christians and churches should redouble their efforts to help pregnant women (some of whom are poor and unwed) carry their babies to birth and find proper parenting, either through assistance in rearing the child or adoption. Already over 4,000 programs and pregnancy shelters (such as Jerry Falwell's Liberty Godparent Ministries) have been established by churches and religious groups. The need for such assistance will be increased when a human life amendment is passed.

If you think a human life amendment is an extreme suggestion, watch the "Living Will" legislation under consideration by the state legislature in Hawaii, the most liberal state in the nation. When first proposed, this legislation offered doctors the right to determine when terminally ill patients could die—without consulting the family. If the humanists try something so bizarre during a conservative revival, can you imagine what they will do if they climb back into the cockpit?

3. Eliminate pornography from both print and video.

Surely a way can be found to protect the constitutional right of free expression, which often shields pornography, and at the same time to defend women against forcible rape and children from molestation and incest, which is often fired by an exposure to pornography or explicit television programs. Since child pornography has been declared illegal, I see no reason why adult porn cannot be similarly labeled.

If conservative courts cannot find a way to declare porn illegal without violating the First Amendment, then the principle of "liberty with responsibility" may prove adequate. For example, a rape victim ought to be able to sue not only her assailant but also the store that sold the magazine, the distributor, and the publisher if a link to the particular magazine can be established. A few such suits could close down the pornography business in a few months. Pornography is only profitable today because publishers do not have to pay for the consequences of the moral holocaust they unleash.

4. Establish a strong national defense.

Government's primary purpose is to protect its citizens from attack, both foreign and domestic. In a world threatened by communism's well-advertised intentions of world conquest, it is the supreme duty of government to arm sufficiently so as to defend citizens against the plight of 40 percent of the rest of the world's population, which today is enslaved by communism. Some conservatives put this at the top of the agenda. I would have no quarrel with that, for if we lose our freedoms to a Communist dictator, we will forfeit our Constitution and all other rights.

5. Adopt a freedom-with-responsibility philosophy.

Government needs to change our criminal justice system from one of leniency to the criminal and minimal concern for the victim to one of protection for the law-abiding population. Since the death penalty has almost been abandoned and legal technicalities have been found to protect criminals from bearing the responsibility for their crimes, America has been turned into the crime capital of the world.

The basic problem stems from the humanist philosophy, adopted by courts and legislators, that society is to blame if citizens steal, rape, and kill. Americans have proved that poverty does not cause crime, since we are the richest people in the world and still have the highest crime rate.

We need a new emphasis on responsibility as the natural partner of freedom. Total freedom does not exist. For example, I am not "free" to drive a car. I must pass a test, possess a license, be responsible for the mechanical condition of my car, drive in the proper direction, proceed at the correct speed, and obey the rules. Otherwise I must pay a fine, go to jail, or lose my right to drive. True liberty is always circumscribed by law. One of our forefathers said that liberty is "the freedom to do that which is right."

If our courts adopted a freedom-with-responsibility philosophy, crime would be extremely unprofitable. Suppose an armed robber shoots a father of three children and is sent to prison. Under this philosophy, the judge and jury would require him to work within the penal system to pay for the support of those children and their mother. After all, the robber killed their means of support; he should be required to replace it. In like manner, the man who rapes a woman and causes her pregnancy should pay for the cost of his crime to both woman and child. Conservatives are not opposed to freedom, but we do favor that it be reasonably balanced with responsibility.

6. Halt deficit spending and eliminate government waste, unnecessary bureaucracy, and uncontrolled spending.

"Buy now and pay later" is contrary to biblical principles. With a national debt in excess of $2 trillion, we must begin to pay for our past. If we do not, we assure poverty for our children.

Since moving to Washington, D.C., I have observed that bureaucracy feeds on itself. We pay government workers who spend their time thinking up schemes that cost taxpayers more money. I sometimes wonder if the country would be better off with 50 percent fewer employees. In fact, as bizarre as it may sound, we could well afford to pay the salaries of 50 percent of our bureaucrats while they seek employment elsewhere. Such a move would save the taxpayer billions of dollars in new schemes and projects that would never be attempted.

Although such a procedure is not likely, almost everyone agrees that government is horrendously wasteful. The well-publicized Peter Grace Report has been largely ignored by government workers, but it still contains 2,478 separate, distinct, and specific . . . cost cutting, revenue-enhancing recommendations for government.

Let me share with you just three of those ideas, which would save the government a total of $63.1 billion and add $4.5 billion to the treasury over a three-year period:

• In the Northwest, the Federal Power Marketing Administration is selling subsidized power at one-third of market rates. If the Federal power were priced at market, there would be a three-year increase in revenues of $4.5 billion, which equates to the three-year personal income taxes of 676,000 median income American families who are thus subsidizing a discrete group in one part of the country. . . .

• The Civil Service and Military Retirement Systems provide to participants three times and six times the benefits, respectively, of the best private sector plans. . . . Modifying major Federal pensions to provide benefits comparable to those of the best private sector plans, slightly better in the case of military pensions, would result in three-year savings of $60.9 billion, equivalent to the three-year income taxes of 9.2 million median income families.

• We found Congressional interference to be a major problem. For example, because Congress obstructs the closing of bases that the military wants to close, the three-year waste is $367 million. In total, PPSS recommends three-year savings of $3.1 billion by closing excess military bases, equivalent to the three-year income taxes of 466,000 median income families.[2]

The Grace Report favors such changes over increasing personal income tax. I believe that most American citizens would agree. A conservative government should resist the temptation of all governments to increase its size, costs, and control over people. We need reduction, not expansion.

7. Change our inept welfare system to an effective people rehabilitation program.

I can remember when President Dwight D. Eisenhower sold the Congress on a Department of Health and Human Services with an annual budget of $5 billion. In 1987 that budget was $292 billion,[3] the third largest in the world (behind only the total U.S. and Soviet Union budgets). This department alone easily accounts for our national debt and has proven vastly inept, expensive, and, in many cases, harmful to the poor. A recent report indicated that the combined costs of welfare for local, state, and national government totals over $600 billion a year—even though we have less than 7 percent unemployment.

Since welfare office centers are usually urban, welfare has contributed to ghettoizing our major cities, where the poor are drawn away from the best job markets to terrible living conditions and a perpetuated dependency on government support. Third-generation welfare recipients are now common. The aid to dependent families, a welcome support for widows and abandoned women with small children, is now a means of livelihood as girls purposely get themselves pregnant for the fourth and fifth time. An inner-city school teacher told me recently that during a discussion of intended vocations one girl told her, "I don't need any more education. I'm planning to get pregnant four or five times, and the government will support me—just like my mother."

An inner-city pastor reported to a group of ministers that welfare was actually encouraging couples to get divorced since two people living separately receive higher monthly payments than do husband and wife. The same is true for some senior citizens who would like to marry but live together out of wedlock because if they marry, retirement checks go down.

Somehow we need to abandon the idea that government owes people a living. Government should not be responsible for people except in emergencies, the threat of violence (foreign or domestic), calamities, or disaster. No American would object to welfare helping disaster victims or widows with children. But unending aid to the able-bodied who refuse to work because they can make more money staying at home is not only a national disgrace and a defrauding of the taxpayer but a crime against the poor, who need to be encouraged.to get out and work. While it may be true that learning skills on the job often provides take-home pay no larger than welfare payments, the individual's self-respect takes a giant step forward.

Over thirty-five years of welfare has produced an unproductive monster that is in dire need of a complete overhaul. Unless it is undertaken soon, our "welfare state" will both bankrupt the nation and destroy the lives of millions of people. Such reform should be tied to rehabilitation. A person who has the capacity to learn a skill should be given an opportunity to try. Temporary help until a normal person becomes self-sufficient is a commendable service of government, but living indefinitely on the federal dole must not be sanctioned.

As our society develops its technical skills during the 1990s, government should tie temporary subsidies to education. Thousands of today's industrial workers—even some very skilled craftsmen—will soon be automated out of jobs. Such individuals should be offered the opportunity to re-educate themselves to make themselves more marketable. Adult education is a permanent necessity. The government would greatly serve its citizens by launching a national advertising campaign to acquaint citizens with adult educational opportunities (much as they use television to recruit service personnel for the military). A few thousand dollars to upgrade the skills of its workers is a proper government investment, for such monies will be returned many times in increased taxes. Unfortunately, welfare payments are often little more than wasted money that creates tragic human dependency.

8. Get the federal government out of education and make the educational process competitive by allowing tuition tax credits or vouchers for parents to use at the schools of their choice.

Ever since the federal government became involved in education, the academic levels of children have dropped. That is typical of government. Everything it touches can be done better by private industry in a competitive market. Because government competes with no one, programs become cumbersome, inefficient, and enormously expensive.

In my book *The Battle for the Public Schools,* I demonstrate that tax vouchers would improve education by making it compete for the approval of its customers—parents! Educators deplore the idea, trying desperately to convince parents that it would ruin education. By contrast it would have the same effect on education that foreign imports have had on the auto industry. In the early seventies, when auto makers were unresponsive to the design desires of the people, Japan met those desires and forced Detroit to follow suit.

If industry can derive tax benefits for buildings and equipment, surely the same principle should apply to a parent who is educating the taxpayers of the 21st century. The better their education, the more taxes they can afford to pay. And if educators had to compete for students within a broad spectrum of private, parochial, and public schools, you can be sure they would please the parents by offering a quality education—or get out of the business. Any government that spends over $260 billion dollars a year on education is in the education business.

We face three central problems with education today: 1) it is based on secular humanism because the educators want it that way; 2) it does not have to compete for student enrollment; and 3) it is not reflective of—or in many cases responsive to—the community where it is located. All of these problems would be altered if we instituted tuition tax credits or a voucher system.

9. Develop greater participation in the political process by Christians and other religiously committed citizens.

If born-again Christians represent "4 out of 10 people" in the population, we ought to aim for 40 percent of the seats in Congress, the cabinet, and other areas of influence in government, media, and education. I am not calling for government quotas, as liberal critics often accuse. We simply need to establish goals on the part of the Christian community and all other citizens who share our religious values. To have the same representation in government as in the population, we should occupy 40 Senate seats and 174 House seats. We should look forward to filling 297 of the 743 federal judgeships and at least 3 Supreme Court posts. Let me repeat, I am not suggesting a religious test for such positions, merely a greater emphasis by preachers, Christian college professors, and other believers on the worthwhile nature of the legal, political, and judicial professions. We need to raise the consciousness level among our Christian youth and professional people to consider such vocations until we gain a representation equal to our numbers in the population.

This same goal should be held by Catholic, Jewish, and other religious citizens also. We would serve future generations well if all religious citizens of the nation became more involved in the political process, not only as candidates but as voters and campaign volunteers. For example, if just 500 such citizens in each congressional district volunteered their services to help elect the candidate who best represented their moral values, we could turn this nation back to moral sanity in one decade—to the benefit of religious Americans.

Time magazine ridiculed me for declaring that a secular humanist is not qualified to hold government office in America. I do not apologize! Unfortunately, secularists have brainwashed our population into thinking that vocational qualifications are primary when we select a political candidate or appointee. Felix Frankfurter, Earl Warren, William O. Douglas, and others may have been well qualified as Supreme Court justices in a secular nation, but all had a harmful effect on the United States judicial system because they did not share our founding fathers' (and the majority of the American people's) commitment to religious values. A person's religious principles—or lack of them—will influence almost every major decision of his life.

A Baptist attorney friend of mine provided a clear illustration of this. He was defending a Christian woman whose homosexual husband was challenging her custody of their teenage son. The first judge, hostile to religion, awarded custody to the father even though the child's environment was one of blatant homosexuality. Somehow during the appeal trial a new judge was assigned to the case, much to the delight of the Baptist attorney, who noted with expectation, "The new judge is a Roman Catholic with five children!" He knew that the judge would be influenced in his legal decisions by strong moral and religious beliefs.

It is time to admit that such a procedure is right and proper. Politicians whose voting records or published positions conflict with traditional values should have no place in a government based on the Judeo-Christian heritage of America. Certainly they are welcome to live here in freedom and enjoy every protection of the law, but the religious people whose taxes provide their salaries and whose votes determine their positions in office have both a right and a duty to elect representation in keeping with their values—regardless of political party.

10. Establish a television network committed to truth and traditional values.

We do not have free media in America but a liberally controlled press and entertainment industry. Although it is less than forty years old, television is becoming increasingly awesome in its influence on the thinking of this nation. I find it ironic that all four networks—ABC, CBS, NBC, and the so-called Public Broadcasting System (PBS)—are overwhelmingly liberal.

We need at least one conservative network to offer an alternative to the liberal bias we are usually confronted with on network newscasts. But the howl sent up by liberals when Senator Jesse Helms launched a legal takeover attempt of CBS is typical of the liberal respect for fairness and freedom. It would be tragic, they clamored, if one conservative network were allowed to "distort" the news. Fairness to them is a score of four to zero. That sounds like thought control to me.

Whether Senator Helms's attempt to change CBS is successful remains to be seen, but at least it is a step in the right direction (no pun intended). Another method could also give the American people more balanced television viewing: breaking up the monopolistic strangle hold of the liberals on the four networks. The government would only have to declare VHF (channels 1–13) obsolete and establish UHF as the official TV signal for the nation. Even after assigning the four networks a spot on the UHF dial, it could open up between ten and twenty frequency possibilities to every city in the country. Competition for new TV stations and national networks would open the door for conservative entrepreneurs to move into this field.

Currently the only real control a viewer exercises over his television is the on-off switch. Making UHF our national TV signal would give viewers another option, for they could turn to one of fifty other stations. (Hopefully cable TV or DBS, Direct Broadcast Satellite, will accomplish this by the year 2000.)

11. Use American technology and agriculture to help the suffering and impoverished throughout the world.

It seems obscene to pay American farmers $21 billion a year *not* to farm while starving people throughout the world are crying for our help. There must be some way to use this money in the purchase of wheat, corn, and other staples so Third World nations friendly to our government could sustain life. If the only reason the American farmer is not free to feed the world is that this action would destroy the world's economy, we need to re-evaluate our national priorities. A people-to-people food program would go a long way toward bettering relations between us and less fortunate nations, and it would save countless numbers of lives. Admittedly there are complications to such a program, but until we adopt an all-encompassing project, the plight of hungry nations will not be remedied.

American technological superiority will undoubtedly create a moral responsibility in the next century that even some of our finest philosophers, theologians, and thinkers have not yet seriously anticipated. Biogenetics could provide food-growing capabilities per acre that would feed an unlimited world population. In addition, space and aquamarine explorations and experiments will have a profound effect on supplying the basic needs of mankind.

Wouldn't it be tragic if we selfishly sat on these blessings and kept them (or sold them) to others? We need some moral thinkers who would declare, Yes, Uncle Sam, you *are* your brother's keeper! Because God has blessed America in an unprecedented way, we need to treat those blessings as Christ did the young lad's lunch, which fed 5,000. Even after the disciples freely dispersed food to this multitude, they discovered that the baskets left over exceeded the original amount!

Perhaps it will take a born-again patriot in the White House to show history what God can do with a nation that is committed to fulfilling His will in truly loving our fellow man as we do ourselves.

I am not suggesting that we turn the entire world into a giant welfare state. We could tie American aid to self-help and local education. Many thorny problems would arise, but how much better to recruit our youth to spend two to four years (or a vocation) in a people-to-people program, teaching the illiterate how to improve their lives, than to recruit them to enter military service or to prepare them for a materialistic future based on "me-ism."

12. Ensure the world's safety from nuclear attack.

Trillions of dollars have been spent by the Communist and non-Communist countries in producing the most frightening military buildup in world history. Today both sides have enough nuclear arms to destroy the world *several* times over. It is now time for the United States to use its technological superiority to protect the world from a universal holocaust. Such a plan, admittedly in its developmental status, is the president's Strategic Defense Initiative (SDI) or Star Wars program. This defense umbrella, or one like it, will have the capacity to destroy incoming missiles out in space long before they can reach their targets and thus render nuclear arms obsolete.

If such a possibility exists, we owe it to the world to develop and use it—not only for our own national protection, but for that of all countries. Through American ingenuity we can implement a program that will make the 21st century free of the constant fear of nuclear destruction. America should be morally strong enough to embark on such a worthy goal.

Many tough moral decisions face our nation in the future, which is why we need some morally tough political leaders to make them. Liberalism and secular humanism will never provide such leadership. Only those whose religious roots are firmly planted in the Judeo-Christian moral absolutes of the Bible will be able to serve as fit representatives of the majority of the American people. But be sure of this: Whoever makes the legislative decisions in the nineties will influence the next century.

13. Reaffirm America as a religious country rather than a secular nation.

For over two hundred years this nation has accommodated religion. Unlike the Communist leaders of the Soviet Union, our forefathers recognized that man is basically a religious creature and that religion is an asset to our nation. That is why we stamp "In God We Trust" on our coins. It is why our presidents, Supreme Court justices, and participants in courts of law swear an oath of integrity or loyalty with their hand upon the Word of God. The noisy liberals who claim that America was not founded on religious principles have never opened a history book or toured our nation's capital, where hundreds of biblical or religious inscriptions appear on our official monuments.

Conservatives do not want a Protestant or Catholic government that uses its power to coerce unbelievers or confuse doctrine with law. Government, however, should not be hostile to religion—as it is rapidly becoming today. Unless this trend is reversed, the small number of secularizers (a term I use to denote those whose goal is to secularize our society) in influential positions will continue to remove our historic religious recognition. It is a tragic distortion of our Constitution and the intent of our founding fathers that Christmas carols must be kept out of public schools and that sexual promiscuity between unwed teens cannot be labeled as immoral (not to mention a health hazard)—all to avoid offending the 6 percent of the nation's atheists. That America is *not* a secular nation needs to be officially reaffirmed. This would not only allow voluntary school prayer but would make it possible for our teachers to introduce character training into their curricula.

14. A Moral-Spiritual Revival

Many conservatives look for a moral revival for our country. Why? Consider these facts:

• At our present rate of homosexual and bisexual activity, 51 percent or more of the population will die of AIDS by the year 2000 if a cure is not found.[4]

• At its present rate of incidence, 15 to 20 percent of our population will have incurable herpes by 1990 unless a cure is discovered.[5]

• More than 1 million high school children are having their own children each year; four out of five are unmarried. Yet authorities are demanding more sex education and more Planned Parenthood, the very things that have compounded the problem during the past twenty years.[6]

• Divorce ravages families. Some estimate that at least 45 million children will spend some time living with only one parent due to divorce before their eighteenth birthdays, and statistics show that children from divorced families are more apt to divorce than those reared by their natural parents.

Most members of the conservative/born-again coalition look for a moral spiritual revival. I am convinced that unless this nation experiences revival similar to the Great Awakening, the United States is doomed to repeat the paths of decadent societies before us. A political revival is not enough. We must have a moral-spiritual revival like those that shook the American society to its very foundations, maintaining an impact on the nation for decades. Calvin Coolidge, our thirtieth president, said, "America was born in a revival of religion. Back of that revival were John Wesley, George Whitefield, and Francis Asbury."[7]

Figure 1, designed by Dr. Don Howard, shows the spiritual cycles of the past and compares them to the one spiritual leaders anticipate. Let's look at these earlier revivals to see what consequences such an awakening could have on our nation.

Figure 1

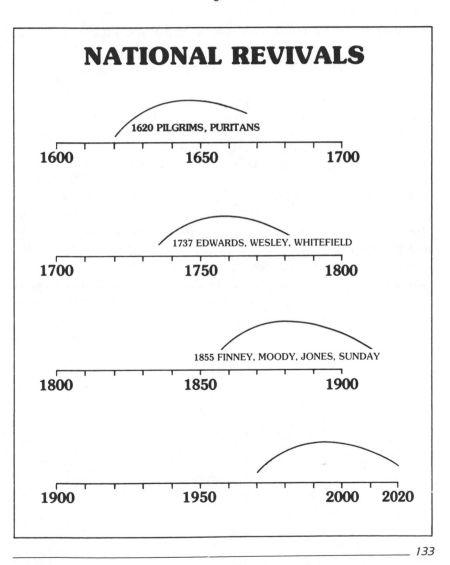

NATIONAL REVIVALS

1620 PILGRIMS, PURITANS

1600   1650   1700

1737 EDWARDS, WESLEY, WHITEFIELD

1700   1750   1800

1855 FINNEY, MOODY, JONES, SUNDAY

1800   1850   1900

1900   1950   2000   2020

At thirty-one, Benjamin Franklin watched the Great Awakening and later described it in his autobiography:

> It was wonderful to see the change soon made in the manners of our inhabitants. From being thoughtless or indifferent about religion, it seemed as if all the world were growing religious, so that one could not walk thro' the town in an evening without hearing psalms sung in different families of every street.[8]

The revival even influenced college campuses. President Willard of Harvard University described the Harvard students after George Whitefield preached in Boston in 1739:

> Gentlemen's sons that were sent here only for a mere polite education are now so full of zeal for the cause of Christ and the love of souls as to devote themselves absolutely to the study of divinity. The college is entirely changed; the students are full of God—and will I hope come out blessings to this and succeeding generations.[9]

This was the atmosphere in which America was born. The people—and their schools and churches and government—were changed. America's revival energized this nation morally and spiritually for over five decades, paving the way for the founding of the greatest nation in the history of mankind.

It is my prayer, and the prayer of every Christian leader I know, that God will once again visit America with a Great Awakening-type revival—just before we race into the 21st century.

8

What If Secular Humanism Wins the Race?

Overthrowing capitalism is too small for us. We must overthrow the whole patriarchy.[1]

By the year 2000 we will, I hope, raise our children to believe in human potential, not God.[2]

Gloria Steinem
Editor, MS. Magazine
Recipient, American Humanist Association Pioneer Award, 1978.

*I*N 1981 I was ridiculed on the front page of the *Washington Post* for suggesting there was a grassroots movement of the American people back toward moral responsibility. Just five years later this same national newspaper admitted that such a movement is indeed spreading across the country. It seems the pendulum swing back to more traditional moral values is so strong that even the liberal media is recognizing the phenomenon. Admittedly the move is not entirely because of the new interest in spiritual values, but it is largely related to the threat of AIDS and other sexually transmitted diseases.

A study conducted by New York research psychologist Srully Blotnick in 1986 found that "casual sex in the USA has declined dramatically since the freewheeling '60s, and fear of sexually transmitted disease is a major reason."[3]

Blotnick surveyed 12,000 single men and women between the ages of 20 and 39 in 1966 and again in 1986. In 1966, 75.3 percent of men and 39.1 percent of women "liked the idea of casual sex." In

1986, only 55.7 percent of men and 23.8 percent of women liked the idea.[4]

Tony Marshall, senior public health educator for San Diego County, sees a similar trend. He predicts, "Basically, what we're getting back to is more and more monogamy. . . . And funny things might start happening in years to come."[5]

These funny things include men and women deciding at an early age that they're going to get married and not have any other sexual partners. "Like it was in the fifties," Marshall predicts. Marshall also cites the spread of AIDS as the reason for this return of sexual mores. He says that some experts claim that the number of AIDS victims in the nation is doubling each year and that the number of heterosexual victims may eventually surpass homosexuals if people do not reduce or eliminate promiscuity.[6]

If AIDS breaks out as a serious threat to the heterosexual community by the turn of the century, it could make sexual commitment in marriage the primary goal of an overwhelming percentage of our population, including our young.

Some people are predicting that a reform movement is already building in our nation—people like my friend, Christian educator Dr. Don Howard, founder of the Accelerated Christian Education

Figure 1

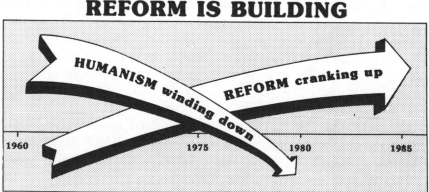

The original concept of Dr. Don Howard, president, Accelerated Christian Education (ACE).

(ACE) school system. Dr. Howard says that a reform movement began to occur around the mid-seventies when fundamentalist Christians and other religious groups began to wake up to the humanist threat in our society. With the election of a conservative president in 1980, humanism began to wane, and a reform movement set in that he predicts will extend into the first two decades of the 21st century. I pray, God, he is right!

Personally I am not so optimistic—perhaps because I view the conflict from my office in Washington, D.C., whereas Don sees it from conservative Dallas, Texas. While it is true that an era of reform has clipped humanism's wings during this decade, the left have certainly not surrendered. They may be winding down, but they are doing everything they can to protract the present period of conflict and reassert themselves before it is too late. The proliferation of new liberal activist groups, along with an attempt on the part of old liberal organizations to enter the race, leads me to believe that the hottest period of conflict will arise during the next decade—1986 through the elections of 1996—which I have labeled the "decade of conflict." The outcome of that election will undoubtedly indicate whose values will prevail during the 21st century.

Figure 2

THE DECADE OF CONFLICT

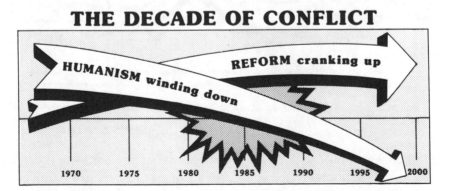

This decade will feature vicious attacks by humanists in education, media (particularly television), government, and many liberal-humanist organizations like NOW, ACLU, P.A.W.,against religion, the Christian church, traditional moral values, and conservative religious leaders.

What if the Left Returns to Power?

Just suppose that President Reagan does not get to appoint two conservatives to the Supreme Court bench (which is necessary to swing that body to conservative control). And just suppose that in the election of 1988, a "moderate" to liberal president were elected and the Senate became as liberal as the present House of Representatives. (Lest you think that could not happen, keep in mind that we are only talking about six people—a president, a vice president, and four senators.) Figure 3 clearly shows the influence this would have on the race for the 21st century and the subsequent impact on the society of the future.

Figure 3

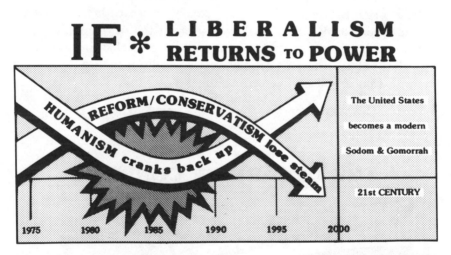

This bleak picture illustrates what could happen if conservatives lose control of Congress, Senate, and White House in 1988, 1992, or 1996. Barring a miracle of God, the future will be decided by the next three national elections.

It does not take a genius to figure out what the left would do if they once again exercised total control of our federal government. Just examine Jimmy Carter's record when he piloted the ship of state, which was a period of great increase in attacks on religious freedom and of growth in secular humanist influence in government and society.

For instance, in 1978 Jerome Kurtz, the Carter-appointed IRS commissioner, proposed sweeping changes in the regulations governing the tax exemptions for Christian schools. Without a public hearing or any public announcement other than an entry in the Federal Register, Kurtz said that Christian schools would have to be racially integrated in their student bodies, faculties, school boards, and even the church boards when the school was sponsored by an individual church to maintain their tax exempt status in 1979.★

This policy was a radical departure from the previous requirements, and Christian leaders asked Kurtz why he had not scheduled a public hearing.

I didn't feel it was that much of an issue, Kurtz replied.

We think it is, the leaders maintained, and a hearing was held in December of 1978. This hearing lasted for four days (twelve hours per day) and was the longest in the history of the IRS. In fact, Jerome Kurtz said that the issue had generated more mail to the IRS offices than any other single issue. What Kurtz thought was not very much of an issue was very important to Christians in our nation. His decision was reversed because Christian leaders were willing to testify against this policy.

What is Secular Humanism?

Liberals purposely try to confuse the general population by making it difficult to define secular humanism. One journalist, who should have known better, suggested that trying to define secular humanism is like trying to nail jello to the wall. Not if you're intellectually honest it isn't!

Secular humanism is the philosophic base of liberalism and is easily defined. I call it a Godless, man-centered philosophy of life that rejects moral absolutes and traditional values. It makes man the measure of all things rather than God. It is usually hostile toward religion in general, with a particular hatred toward Christianity. I consider this world view to be the most harmful, anti-American, anti-Christian philosophy in our country today. Most of society's

★According to Dr. Paul Kienel, president of the Association of Christian Schools International, 80 percent of all Christian schools are church-sponsored.

current evils can be traced to secular humanist thinkers or liberals whose theories originated in that philosophy. It did not originate in America but was transplanted here principally from France and Germany. Its advocates have relentlessly sought to secularize our once religious nation. Secular humanists disagree with the traditional, moral, or religious people on almost every issue of life, from abortion to freedom.

In order to foresee what might happen to our country under a humanistic government, we need to understand the difference be-

Figure 4

The humanist view of the role of government

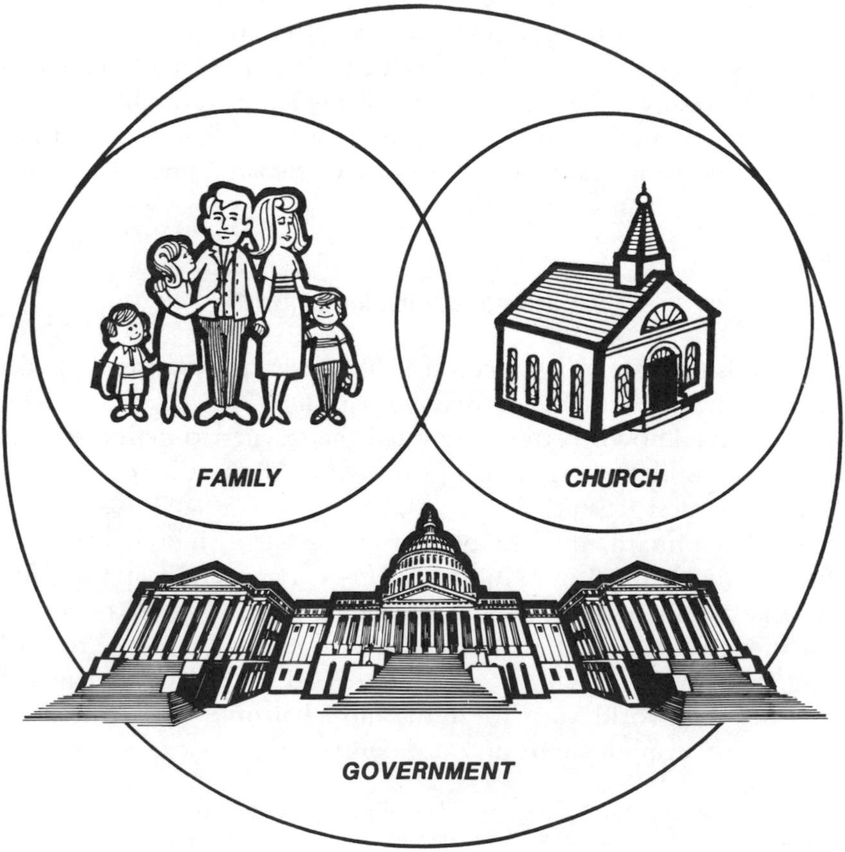

FAMILY

CHURCH

GOVERNMENT

tween the traditional view of the role of government and the view of modern humanists.

The Humanist View of Government

Figure 5 shows the traditional view of the role of government. Although some areas of concern overlap and therefore require mutual cooperation, the traditional view sees all three institutions as essentially separate.

Figure 5

The traditional view of the role of government

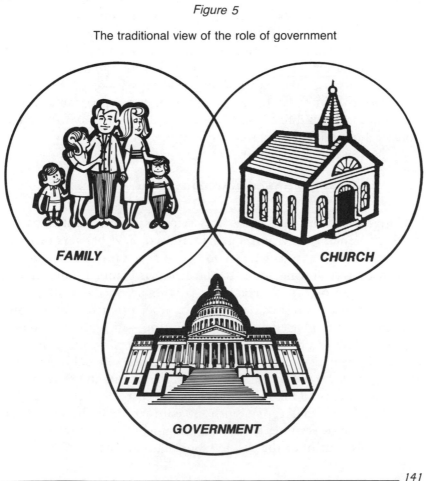

FAMILY

CHURCH

GOVERNMENT

Contrast this view with the humanist view in figure 4. Unfortunately humanists and many liberals believe that government should control everything in society, including the family and the church. If liberals ever take total control of our federal government, I predict this view will serve as their blueprint for the 21st century.

I believe that God intended both government and the church to befriend and support the family. Under humanist control our government has become the enemy of the family (for a full explanation of this, see my book *The Battle for the Family*). Government-controlled schools are often a source of conflict between young people and their parents since they teach secular humanistic values rather than the more traditional values of their parents. Our government has driven many wives and mothers out of the home and into the work force against their will because the tax bite has exceeded 42 percent of the family's earnings (expect that to increase in the years ahead, no matter who is in control of the government). Liberals intend to increase taxes, according to Walter Mondale's 1984 election platform, in order to lavish more on social programs. Some conservatives would likewise raise taxes but only to pay off the national debt and avoid eventual bankruptcy.

What about the Rights of Parents?

Currently government gives lip service to parental control by requiring parental permission if a girl wishes to have her ears pierced. But humanists have usurped control of that same child's sexual choices by transferring them to the schools, Planned Parenthood, and abortion doctors. Today many parents are incensed that their children can be taught about intercourse, outfitted with contraceptives, and advised to seek an abortion—all without parental approval. Interestingly enough, if the child gets venereal disease, becomes pregnant out of wedlock, or develops suicidal depression after an abortion the parents knew nothing about, the bureaucrats want the parents to take responsibility again.

If liberals do that today without command of the executive branch of our government, can you imagine what they would do if they gained control of the White House? Government social workers might make all the decisions for children, since liberals and humanists tend to consider children the property of government, not parents. Every religious and morally responsible parent has a vital stake in the leaders who run our government, for parents could lose control of the destiny of their children before the next century just by electing a liberal president and more liberal senators.

What about Public Education?

If a liberal administration came to power, they would welcome secular humanists back into the federal Department of Education, which would assume even greater control over education than it now possesses. If we find it difficult to get anything but evolution taught in public schools today, what do you suppose it would be like if government were totally controlled by liberals who favor secular humanism? The humanists themselves have already told us in an article, "A Religion for a New Age" in the official organ of the American Humanist Association, _The Humanist_ magazine:

> I am convinced that the battle for humankind's future must be waged and won in the public school classroom by teachers who correctly perceive their role as the proselytizers of a new faith: a religion of humanity that recognizes and respects the spark of what theologians call divinity in every human being. These teachers must embody the same selfless dedication as the most rabid fundamentalist preachers. For they will be ministers of another sort, utilizing a classroom instead of a pulpit to convey humanist values in whatever subject they teach, regardless of the educational level—preschool day care or large state university. The classroom must and will become an arena of conflict between the old and the new—the rotting corpse of Christianity, together with all its adjacent evils and misery, and the new faith of humanism, resplendent in its promise of a world in which the never-realized Christian ideal of "love thy neighbor" will finally be achieved.[7]

From _Today's Education,_ the National Education Association journal, comes this statement: "The basic role of the teacher will change noticeably. Ten years hence it should be more accurate to term him a 'learning clinician.' This title is intended to convey the idea that schools are becoming 'clinics' whose purpose is to provide individualized psychosocial 'treatment' for the student. . . ."[8]

No wonder the schools are doing such a poor job of teaching the basics. "Clinicians" don't teach; teachers do!

At an education seminar for about a thousand teachers, Dr. Chester Pierce, a Harvard University professor of education and psychiatry, announced:

> Every child in America entering school at the age of five is mentally ill because he comes to school with certain allegiances toward our founding fathers, toward our elected officials, toward his parents, toward a belief in a supernatural being, toward the sovereignty of this nation as a separate entity. . . . It's up to you teachers to make all of these sick children well by creating the international children of the future.[9]

This statement was confirmed in essence as reflecting his beliefs by an attorney friend of mine through a personal telephone call to the professor. Keep in mind that the man is an educator of educators.

Secular humanists are embarrassed when we publicize statements like this so they deny that such comments reflect the majority opinion of their group. In fairness, these statements may represent an extreme. But if they are so blatant when the left is no longer in total control, what, pray tell, would they do if they dominated our federal government?

Don't be misled by the humanist call for "freedom and liberty." They simply mean that humanists and liberals must have the freedom and liberty to teach their doctrines at the taxpayers' expense, and we Christians have the liberty and freedom to pay taxes, keep our mouths shut, and stay out of politics. If the humanists ever regain control of the White House and Senate, I am convinced that religious citizens and fundamentalists, in particular, will enjoy about as much freedom as a creationist biology teacher now has in the public school classroom.

What about Religious Freedom?

If liberals gain effective control of our federal government, I shudder to think of their impact on religious freedom. First will come a concerted attempt to confine religious expression to the church and home. That will curtail both personal and mass evangelism. Then they will institute licensing of preachers by the state, with limitations, of course, placed on ministers who wish to get involved in politics. Eventually the church's influence will be much the same as it is presently in Communist countries.

The Electric Church

One of the first religious freedoms to disappear would be the electric church. Because of their hatred for religion (Christianity in particular) and their fear that television and radio ministers can awaken a sufficient number of listeners to wrest the control of government, media, and education from them, the humanists will find some way to get us all off the air. Already we have seen news and sports programs replacing many religious programs on Sunday morning for two major reasons. One, for years many stations sold time to religious programmers only because they were the sole buyers of Sunday morning air time, not because the media cared for the message. Now other buyers are entering the market. Two, the networks are beginning to charge so much that many religious programmers cannot raise enough money to stay on the air. If the left return to power, they will find some reason to justify banning all religious radio and telecasting.

Fortunately, four religious cable networks are already owned by Christians, another is starting, a direct broadcasting network will soon be introduced, and a new conservative cable network is on the drawing boards. In addition, technology is in our favor; new means of communicating with the average household are becoming operational so rapidly that it may not be possible for any except the most totalitarian government to shield people from truth as Orwell's _Newspeak_ did.

Good-bye Bulk Mail

Another freedom I expect to be sacrificed if the left ever returns to total power is bulk mail. As we have noted, "junk mail" is the educational and financial lifeline of both the conservative movement and the electric church. Already some in government want to raise the prices of this presorted bulk mail even though postage is now so high that some direct mail programs are no longer financially feasible. If more repressive measures were instituted by a liberal government, it could prove disastrous to the reform movement.

The Race for Sodom and Gomorrah

If the left somehow turn their growing unpopularity into a victory at the polls, we may well experience a return to libertine living before the 21st century. If that happens, I predict that abortions will increase (at government expense); pornographers will be given even greater liberties; television programs will become more perverse; music will degenerate; MTV, cable, and high tech will be used to further break down the values of family life; divorce will skyrocket; and the country will go bankrupt as the result of the big-spending policies of liberalism. Free enterprise will be stifled by Big Brother government regulations imposed by bureaucrats who know little of business and the free market, and taxes will increase until 90 percent of the married women appear in the work force—if jobs are available. Such a forecast is not pleasant, but it is realistic, based on liberal policies from 1932 to 1980.

Who Will Win the Race?

The winner of the race for the 21st century is anyone's guess. The Christian-Conservative Right outnumbers the Humanist-Liberal Left by as much as three to one. But the Supreme Court and both houses of Congress are currently governed by liberals. When we add that liberals own and operate an incredible number of daily newspapers, weekly magazines, the four major networks, and the two wire services, it is easy to understand how they could deceive enough voters to take control of the White House if conservatives put up a weak candidate for president in any national election. If that happens prior to either the Supreme Court or one of the Houses of Congress shifting to conservative control, the result *may* be irreversible.

The next major battle in the war between these two ideologies will occur once "the great communicator" Ronald Reagan is no longer eligible to run for president. Who will be his successor? A moderate-conservative like Vice President George Bush or an aggressive conservative like Congressman Jack Kemp? Or will it be a Christian leader like Pat Robertson, whose well-publicized consideration of such a possibility has stirred up considerable interest both inside religious ranks and in secular politics?

A Minister for President?

Christian leaders frequently debate the issue. Should a minister of the gospel run for public office—specifically the highest office of the land? Why not? Many of God's most faithful servants in the Old Testament were political leaders: Moses, Joshua, Samuel, Daniel, David, and others.

Pat Robertson, of course, is extremely well qualified. 1) He has a deep commitment to God and the traditional values of America. 2) He was reared by a United States senator father, holds a Yale law degree, is an extremely successful businessman, and thoroughly knowledgeable about foreign affairs (with a particular awareness of the Middle East). 3) He is a man of integrity. Politicians are trusted by the American people just two steps above used-car salesmen, who finished last in a survey of twenty-four professions. Ministers were first. Although the media will not admit it, many Americans would vote for a minister just to elect a president they can trust. 4) Pat Robertson is a master communicator. Twenty-three years of television experience on his daily "700 Club" have given him exposure to more people than any other candidate except the vice president. In television charisma he is just a step or two behind "the great communicator."

Pat Robertson may not run in 1988. He will probably make that decision a few months after this book is published. But I find it exciting that the most watched TV minister in the nation is even considering the possibility. That should help to break the self-imposed boycott of public service (both elective and civil service) that has plagued Christians for over fifty years, legitimizing politics as a meaningful vocation for Christians. If Pat Robertson runs for president in '88, I predict he will open the floodgates for many thousands of Christians to run for every office in the land—from local school boards to city councils and state legislatures. This trend will carry over into the 21st century and will influence the moral climate of America for the next fifty years.

There Is No Substitute for Victory!

I believe that the majority of the people in this country can be made to understand the threat to their freedoms from a return to liberalism so that they will see that we have no alternative but to win this race! The trends are in our favor, since the mood of the country during the past decade or so, particularly under President Reagan, is flowing back toward traditional values. Citizens committed to traditional values are beginning to run for elective offices. Some are starting to move up to federal positions. If this trend continues for one more decade, conservatism will be the wave of the 21st century. Religious freedom will be assured, and the ship of state will gradually turn toward the traditional values President Reagan

Figure 6

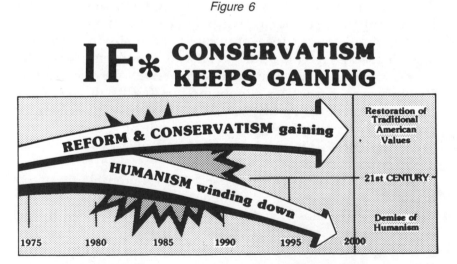

This rosy projection depends on more conservative victories particularly in Congress, the Senate, and the White House in 1988, 1992, and 1996.

has talked about for twenty years. Traditional values could be taught once again in our public schools. Television would be required to adhere to moral standards and would once again become fit for family viewing. Such a victory is worth our most strenuous efforts.

I have found that the most difficult part of a race occurs at the 75 percent mark. When I ran my first 10K race (six miles), the fourth and fifth miles almost killed this three-mile-a-day jogger. The sixth mile was easy, for the goal was in sight and the adrenalin was pumping. The mid-eighties represent that fourth mile, the early nineties the fifth mile. If we keep working, we are probably only one decade away from that victorious last mile. *This is no time to quit!* The election of 1996 will tell the story.

In order to win the race, we need two dynamic levels of participation. First, we must encourage Christians to run for every office in the land, from school boards (about 80,000 positions), to city council members, county supervisors, state legislators (about 7,000 offices), governors, representatives to the national House of Representatives, and senators. Second, we need to recruit 500 to 1,000 dedicated Christians in each of the 435 congressional districts and give them the training necessary to campaign effectively on behalf of a candidate who shares their values. This would change the complexion of both the House and the Senate for years to come.[9]

In 1 Corinthians 9:24–27 the apostle Paul offers the best advice to all believers contending in life's race:

> Do you not know that those who run in a race all run, but one receives the prize? Run in such a way that you may obtain it.
>
> And everyone who competes for the prize is temperate in all things. Now they do it to obtain a perishable crown, but we for an imperishable crown.
>
> Therefore I run thus: not with uncertainty. Thus I fight: not as one who beats the air.
>
> But I discipline my body and bring it into subjection, lest, when I have preached to others, I myself should become disqualified.

But Life Goes On

In a ten-to-fifteen-year race, which is what we are talking about, you will continue to eat, sleep, work, marry, raise children, and exercise your personal will in relation to God hundreds of times. Our Lord indicated that such activities would persist until His Second Coming (Matthew 24:37). Whether conservatives control the future or liberals regain their domination, the secularizing, antimoral influence of liberal humanism over the past fifty years will continue to affect our society.

Cultural change takes place slowly, so a wise Christian must understand that he is really racing on two fronts at the same time. To change the future, he must fight the forces that are misshaping society. But he must also protect himself and his family from those liberal-humanist influences in society that are already trying to destroy it. It will do your family little good if you neglect it to win the race for our culture in the next century. The rest of this book is dedicated to helping you prepare for the 21st century—in your vocational, spiritual, and domestic life.

STEP FOUR

Prepare Yourself and Your Family

9

What New Vocational Training Might You Need?

Jobs are changing so fast there is no way schools can train students that far in advance. We need to graduate students who know what are the best ways to use the new technology and are capable of learning new skills.[1]

Michael Timpane, President
Columbia University Teachers College

THE individual who fails to plan for the electrifying changes that will appear in the immediate future may be in danger of becoming unemployable. Many professions will be automated out of existence. If robots don't replace the person on the assembly line or in the manufacturing plant, the tasks will either be performed in a Third-World country much more cheaply, or new high-tech inventions will make a present vocation altogether obsolete.

We must learn a lesson from farmers, steelworkers, and textile workers. At one time in this country 80 percent of our population worked on the farm. Today that has been reduced to 7 percent, and by the year 2000 it will only be 3 percent. Many farmers have fallen on such hard times that even $21 billion a year in government subsidies cannot make their profession profitable. Science and technology have combined to give such high yields per acre and such rapid harvesting that supply far exceeds demand for basic foods.

Obviously, if most of the nation's farmers do not learn new skills during this decade, they will be unemployable before the end of the decade. The same can be said for hundreds of other vocations, particularly the unskilled.

Textile and shoe companies are facing a similar dilemma. Third-World countries—where unions and government-guaranteed minimum wages are nonexistent—produce these products so much cheaper than we do that foreign companies can afford the expense of shipping their products here and still undersell American producers. "David L. Birch reports that, as of May 1983, only 12 percent of our labor force is engaged in manufacturing operations today."[2]

A look at past history already shows a significant decline. The federal government's Bureau of Labor statistics reported that over 1.6 million manufacturing jobs were eliminated between 1979 and 1984. Within a decade an unskilled laborer or workman in the trades or manufacturing industries may find himself competing with ten or more other people for every available job.

I can remember when we felt that the United States could supply the entire world with manufactured steel. No more! Between union insistence upon higher wages, environmentalists' demands for high-cost pollution controls, and the failure of the United States steel companies to switch to new high-tech methods of manufacturing, it is now possible for other countries to manufacture steel and ship it into our country, underselling our producers. Don't be surprised if we have little or no steel industry by the year 2000.

The ever-growing fast food industry, which employs many un-skilled workers, is also targeted for change. Test experiments in which a six-armed robot delivers orders are already underway in six fast-food outlets. Futurists predict that one day soon you will give your order to a voice-activated computer (or push a few buttons) at the drive-up window and then watch robots shift into action to prepare your food. After you receive your order on a sanitized delivery belt, a mechanical voice will announce, "Thank you for shopping at _____" (your favorite junk food outlet)!

These are only some of the many vocations that were stable during the first three quarters of this century but may be obsolete before it ends.

Stephen Cohen, professor of business at the University of California at Berkeley, warned, "By 1995, there will only be high-tech industries in this country, . . . whether they make pants, motors, insurance policies or microchips."[3] That may be a bit hyperbolic, for we will always need someone to service the robots. But it is no exaggeration to affirm that by the turn of the century, 85 percent of the population will be in the business of information or services. During the 1980s, as our government continues to learn that free enterprise does better without its "help," a groundswell of self-employed entrepreneurism will continue to spark millions of small businesses and offer thousands of new jobs. The key to holding a job in the future will be 1) a good basic education, including math and computers; 2) continuing progress in education; and 3) a willingness to work hard or serve people.

Some Jobs of the Future

Currently some of the best vocational opportunities are offered to engineers, computer programmers, systems analysts, fiber optics technicians, electrical technicians, and health care specialists. The Bureau of Labor Statistics forecasts that 90 percent of the new jobs of the future will be in services rather than manufacturing.

A golden opportunity for those who don't feel an aptitude for high tech but love people lies in the health service industry. Technology is prolonging life and biotechnology may even lengthen the current average lifespan of seventy-four for men and seventy-nine for women by another ten years or more before the turn of the century. It is estimated that 23 percent more doctors and surgeons will be needed by 1995. That will require between 30 and 40 percent more nurses, therapists, technicians, aides, and social workers.

Changes in Key Industries

The 1985 reports from the Bureau of Labor Statistics forecast significant changes in key industries during the next decade.

Figure 1

Changes in Key Industries 1984 to 1995[4]

VOCATION	JOBS IN 1984	EXPECTED JOBS BY 1995	% CHANGE OVER 1984
Computers, Electronics	1,155,000	1,559,000	+35%
Health Services	6,559,000	8,332,000	+29%
Hi Tech	6,039,000	7,730,000	+28%
Leisure/ Recreation Services	1,201,000	1,525,000	+27%
Printing & Publishing	1,459,000	1,751,000	+20%
Banking, Finances	4,809,000	5,723,000	+19%
Communications	1,355,000	1,585,000	+17%
Retailing	18,351,000	21,287,000	+16%
Public Utilities	1,042,000	1,177,000	+13%
Auto Manufacturers	863,000	828,000	−4%
Food & Beverage	1,638,000	1,474,000	−10%
Textile & Apparel	1,928,000	1,581,000	−18%

Chart adapted from statistics "Jobs of the Future," *U.S. News & World Report,* December 23, 1985, 40–44.

The same reports suggest that paralegals will increase 98 percent in the next decade. John Naisbitt predicts that we are becoming a "litigious society," and some believe we will see a rise in attorneys from the 650,000 of today to three-quarters of a million by the year 2000.

I foresee an increase in Christian service workers as the Born-again Megatrend continues to gather momentum. An added number of pastor-teachers, missionaries, youth workers, Christian education directors, Christian school teachers, administrators, and specialists will swell the ranks of church workers, necessitating an increase in Bible college and seminary professors to train them.

There will certainly be a continuing need for quality teachers who can equip others, since high-tech advances will require that education become an ongoing, lifetime pursuit. There will always be a need for quality teachers who motivate students to learn, if not in the public or private schools, at least in tutoring those students who missed something in the educational process. One self-employed teacher charges twenty-eight dollars an hour for private instruction and usually teaches three students at a time. Entrepreneurial teachers will hang out their shingles and teach remedial reading, math, writing, and computers, much as music teachers of the past taught piano lessons.

As I noted earlier in the book, creative activities like writing, art, architecture, and computer work can often be done more cheaply at home than in expensive office buildings. It is more economical for a company to outfit an employee with a computer terminal in his home so he can communicate with the company computer by telephone line than to rent space and purchase office equipment. The employee saves driving time and costs, plus other fringe benefits.

The one element that seems to slow the eventual growth of the cottage industry is the isolation of the workers. Even though they enjoy working at home, they miss the contact with friends at the office. Some companies are moving to one-day-a-week department conferences to give employees the human contact they need. Individuals, of course, differ; loners can work at home more comfortably than those who are more gregarious.

The cottage industry is a perfect working situation for mothers. Not only can housewives keep their skills sharpened by working part-tme at home, but many working mothers find it more profitable. Studies have shown that by the time the average working wife pays for child-care services, increased income taxes, clothes and lunches, transportation, and other costs necessitated by her working in the marketplace, she only increases the family income about 12–30 percent.

Many wives in the future will find it more profitable to work part-time at home—not only financially but for the good of the entire family. Two working parents put a strain on any family, particularly during the first five years of a child's life. The trend to get mother back into the marketplace within three to six months after the birth of a child is declining. Women are rebelling at being cheated out of the opportunity to become the central persons in their young children's lives; they are returning to mothering as their primary vocation during these early years. This healthy trend will pay great dividends in the emotional development of children.

Correcting a Misconception

The notion that a woman in her mid-to-late thirties is not employable if she has devoted herself to mothering and homemaking for fifteen to twenty years is not realistic. Industry finds that such women often bring organizational skills that cannot be taught in college into the marketplace. My wife, who heads the largest women's organization in the country, is a good example. One day I complimented her skills as an organizer and manager of people. She responded, "You can't raise four children without being a good checker-upper."

One corporation president told me about the success of a woman in his firm. This forty-five-year-old woman had just been elevated to a key position after about seven years in the company. When the president learned that she had had no training or previous experience, he asked the personnel manager why he had hired her in the first place.

The man sheepishly replied, "She charmed me during the interview with the challenge that she could do the job. I had confronted her with the fact that she possessed no skills or experience to offer our firm, so I asked if she could give me one good reason to hire her."

She responded, "Yes, I can get the meat, vegetables, and potatoes on the table all at the same time while they are still hot."

The personnel manager identified organizational ability in this homemaker and mother that paid off for his company.

Self-Discipline the Key

In the past, unions and government protection made it difficult to fire the inefficient employee. Business and government have literally paid people for doing little or nothing. But that is changing! Workers are demanding to be paid for productivity. However, that demand requires self-discipline, an almost obsolete trait. In the future working men and women will experience increasing pressure to develop self-discipline and good work habits. These characteristics can be learned by any individual who has formulated a goal and keeps his mind fixed on it. Someone has observed, "The mind is a goal-striving mechanism." We should train our young to establish proper goals and discuss them frequently so that they stand out clearly in their minds.

Christians should have a distinct advantage, since we are taught in Scripture to discipline ourselves (1 Cor. 9:24–27), and we have the Holy Spirit to give us the gift of self-discipline (Gal. 5:22–23). I have found, however, that we must cooperate with the Holy Spirit in order to utilize that gift. As we walk in His control and do everything to the glory of God (Col. 3:16–17), it is easier to maintain consistency in our spiritual lives and in our work.

Education Is an Ongoing Experience

In this high-tech age, we must consciously revise the concept that we complete our education at the end of a set period. My father quit school after the eighth grade, like many others in the 1920s. In my generation there was a strong emphasis on attending college. Today most collegians aim for graduate school, yet it is becoming inaccurate to consider the Ph.D. "a terminal degree." Today the Ph.D. or M.D. who does not continue the educational process may be obsolete within five years.

An attorney friend of mine is one of the nation's authorities on tax law. He spends 15 percent of his time keeping up with changes in his field. Can you imagine the time he will spend learning the 1,300 pages of Congress's new tax revisions if they pass? The more technical the subject, the more time a person must spend maintaining vocational competence. That is why seminars, conferences, and weekend training sessions have become a booming business.

Somehow we must train our young to look forward to learning as an exciting process, which will require a portion of their time as long as they live—unless they want to be by-passed by the information revolution. The division of life into three states during the industrial age—the learning years (0–22), the working years (22–65), and the retirement years (an average of 5 to 10 years)—will soon become obsolete. Instead, the learning years will be ongoing. The president's chief of staff, Don Regan, left a lifetime vocation on Wall Street at sixty-two to enter the high pressure environment of the White House. At this writing he is sixty-seven and shows every indication of finishing out the president's term of office. Like our president and supreme court justices, many self-employed businessmen plan to work into their eighties. All of these people have one trait in common: the ability to keep on learning throughout life.

The most miserable senior citizens I meet are those whose only option at sixty-five is retirement. The fun-in-the-sun crowd may photograph well for *Leisure World* postures, but one can only enjoy so many cruises and golf games. Besides, leisure activities are expensive and can usually only be afforded by working people. Experts indicate that longer work years, not shorter, are in store for those who remain on the cutting edge of their profession.

I look for the small business, the cottage industry, and changes in profession to become more popular with seniors. For instance, I have a friend who went into the restaurant business two weeks after he retired. Recently I heard Dr. Lehman Strauss preach in Dallas. When he indicated that he "has been married for fifty-five years," I judged that he must be seventy-five or more years of age (though he doesn't look it). I thought his message was better than when I heard him six years ago. During the 21st century, retirement will probably advance from age sixty-five to seventy or eighty.

Adult education in some form is here to stay! Humanly speaking, it is a vital key to vocational longevity, productivity, and enjoyment. Take all the training in your field that you can, and don't limit God's use of your life. With His help, you can be all God wants you to be.

10

How Can You Prepare Your Children?

DURING the past thirty years our culture has been extremely antagonistic toward the traditional family, making it more difficult than at any other time in American history to rear children to love and serve God. On top of this, parents must prepare their children to live in a society that only exists in the minds of today's scientists.

Imagine the advances that our children will encounter! Just as we watched Neil Armstrong step on the moon, they will witness the establishment of space laboratories with people actually living and working in outer space or under the sea. The technological explosion of the past two decades will accelerate rather than slow down, influencing every person on earth, particularly those living in the most advanced high-tech country in the world.

Finally, the family structure of the present and future, which is much more complicated than the traditional family, adds an extra pressure upon family life. In order to help you prepare your family for the future, I would like to review this structure for you. After that, I will suggest ten ways you can prepare your family (whatever its composition might be) for this exciting, though complex, future.

Four Kinds of Families

A survey of one hundred prominent marriage and family counselors asked these professionals to appraise the direction of family life in years to come. A consensus of their findings, which confirms my own observations as a pastor, enables us to envision the family structure of the future. Four kinds of adult families will be prevalent in the next decades: (1) first-marriage or traditional families, (2) single-parent families, (3) remarried families, and (4) single adults.

The Traditional Family

When the Bible speaks about the family, it always addresses the traditional family: one man and one woman, committed to each other so long as they shall live, and their children by marriage or adoption. Today 62 percent or 50 million families fit this category—or once did.

The traditional family may be battered and bent by the forces of materialism and secularism, but it will not cease to exist. After all, our Lord predicted that people would be "marrying and giving in marriage" right up to the time of His coming. History demonstrates that the family is required for civilization to exist, since all cultures that discard the family eventually become extinct.

I look for the Conservative/Born-again Megatrends to swing the pendulum back toward the family in the next decades. Christian families that have been influenced by today's standards will once again return to the biblical principles that have served the family so well during the past two millennia.

The Single-Parent Family

During the last twenty years the divorce rate has more than doubled. Three-fifths of families separated by divorce have children who live at home, and this figure does not include widows or unmarried mothers with children. Only one-tenth of these single-parent families are headed by fathers who rear their children, according to this survey, and this figure is not expected to increase measurably before the turn of the century. Ninety percent of single-parent families are supported by women, and only 43 percent of those mothers receive any financial help from the children's fathers. Single-parent families are often the poorest families in the community.

Twice-Married Families

Seventy-five percent of those who divorce remarry, over 50 percent within three years after their divorce. The remarried family usually creates more problems than it solves. If both spouses bring children to the marriage, life becomes very complex. The sad joke that "My kids and your kids are fighting with our kids" is not funny to the remarried.

Twelve percent of the families in this country (approximately 15 million) are composed of twice-married couples. Talk about adjustment! Imagine two sets of children waiting for the bride and groom to return from the honeymoon. The man and wife may bring a greater motivation to succeed in the second marriage, but his children and her children and their children will present problems never faced by traditional families.

The adjustment period for such couples is all but nonexistent. From the first day, the family constitutes a man and woman trying to relate to each other as one clan is learning to live with another. Sibling jealousy and hostility can complicate matters severely. Statistically, there is a slightly higher divorce rate among the remarried than among the first-married.

Single-Person Households

The last projected family structure of the future has existed for centuries but has significantly increased in recent years, since young men and women are delaying marriage for many reasons. A survey in 1980 revealed that 20 percent of the adult population lived alone. This included the widowed, the elderly, young singles, divorced persons without children, and those who have never married. In some areas of our country, the big cities like New York, Chicago, and Los Angeles, single-person households comprise 30 percent of the population.

The suggestions I will make for families in the coming decades are directed to the first three family structures, which involve one or two parents and one or more children. These ten ideas are designed to help Christian families prepare for the future.

1. Make sure your children master the three basics of education: READING, WRITING, and MATH.

The humanists in education made the dreadful decision years ago that the three R's were no longer relevant. Consequently, 60 million adults are "functionally illiterate," and additional millions find reading difficult. In addition, rote learning was frowned upon; therefore, memorization of multiplication tables and the parts of speech were not emphasized. Today some of the victims of this humanistic educational system are themselves teachers. That this has produced an alarming decline in SAT scores is bad enough, but it is tragic in an era of high-tech explosion, when there is an even greater need for these basic building blocks of learning.

If a computer employee cannot read well, he will always need personal help in solving new problems, for he will not be able to understand the operator's manual. If an engineer cannot write intelligently, he will limit his advancement capabilities by the reports he turns in. A student who does not understand basic math will block out whole vocational areas, many of which would have satisfied his natural aptitudes.

If you wish to guarantee your child's unlimited vocational potential, help him master the basics. Make sure he reads rapidly, with strong retention. Children are curious by nature, and if they learn to be good readers they will amaze you with the number of books they can read. Charlie "Tremendous" Jones, a well-known Christian motivational speaker, has challenged thousands of parents to offer financial rewards to children for reading a book. When children get older, add the requirement of writing a report. And if they don't know how to write a book report, teach them. One drawback to our system of education, either public or Christian, is that we implement reading and writing only to satisfy the requirements of the teacher. For that reason Charlie Jones has introduced the concept "reading for profit." (He gives his children $10 for a completed book report.) The next step will be reading for pleasure. Note the steps of this sequence: 1) reading for learning, 2) reading for profit, 3) reading for pleasure.

I stress reading because I consider it the foundation of all learning. If a child can read well, he can learn almost anything. If he is a poor reader, he will probably find the educational process difficult.

Once your child is well on the road of reading fundamentals, help him with spelling, writing, and math. We used the flash-card system to drill our children. It certainly paid off with our sons: one majored in business and started his own computer company, while the other became an accountant and works with computers constantly. Such home training will be even more essential for young families of the future than it was for mine.

You might even want to enroll your children in a Christian school or consider home schooling, which is becoming increasingly popular, particularly with parents who cannot afford private school tuition or those who wish to be the principal teaching influence during the early lives of their children.

2. Make friends with the computer!

When computers first came out, they were mysterious and complex. Like most parents, I was afraid of them and considered them too difficult to learn. Consequently, I ignored them for many years.

Today they are invading the home. A wise parent who can afford it welcomes one into the home for use as an educational tool for the entire family. Free enterprise has brought the computer's price down to the point that the average family can now afford one. A number of inexpensive software packages can help you in the learning process with your children. Instead of using the old three-by-five flash cards, your children can learn math, vocabulary words, the parts of speech, and almost anything on the family computer, while at the same time becoming friends with the machine. There is a good likelihood that when your child joins the work force, a computer terminal will be sitting on his desk. He might as well make friends with it at home.

Our grandchildren have an Apple II in their home, and all three of them use it regularly. My wife went into the local computer store and overheard them discussing the next software package they were going to buy and some they planned to give as Christmas gifts. Bev commented, "They were talking a language that I did not understand. Computer people have a vocabulary of their own." And she is right—but it really isn't all that difficult. You and your family can learn it a little at a time.

By the 21st century we will probably have computer-activated television capabilities by telephone line. People will be able to shop at home by computer, and even the friendly newspaper boy, a stable part of life for most of this century, will be replaced by electronic delivery of the newspaper to your home computer. The paper will be printed on your own printer as you drink your computer-activated coffee. You will probably cook by computer, and the cars of the future will be safer because they will be controlled by computers instead of humans. (I just hope they will develop a computerized method to help me keep track of my car keys.)

3. Make your home an educational center for your children.

During the days of the industrial revolution, the home was the principal source of education. Children attended the local school eight or nine months of the year to learn the basics, but they learned to work with their hands in the home. Girls were trained in cooking, sewing, and other household duties; boys were taught farming, milking, house repairs, auto mechanics, woodworking, and many other skills. During the industrial age, most manufacturing processes were performed by expensive equipment, which could only be purchased by companies for their factories and corporate offices.

Now, parents will again have the opportunity to prepare their children for the future by giving them a working and playing experience with electronic and computerized gadgetry.

Different skills will be necessary for 21st-century citizens, but thoughtful parents can best prepare their children by themselves keeping up with as many advanced high-tech inventions as possible. Family field trips and outings should encompass more than just sports and recreation. They should include trips to places like the Epcot Center at Disneyworld, electronic fairs, and computer shows or displays where children can get a one- or two-day education about the future. Watch your local paper for announcements of such events. Remember, learning does not only take place in the classroom or a formal learning center. Sea World, Space World, and Futurama can be entertaining, interesting, and profitable learning experiences. They may even spark a new level of learning curiosity in your child's mind.

4. Schedule times for family togetherness.

One of the advantages of the cottage industry is that parents and children will be forced to spend more time together. This will remedy the social problem that has grown during the early days of the information revolution (approximately 1955 to the present). Some busy parents are fortunate to be able to eat the evening meal with the family, with only one or two hours a night for family fellowship. Unfortunately, everyone seems to have activities and responsibilities that curtail time with the family. The only effective way to deal with that problem is to establish workable schedules.

A while ago Bev and I were invited to have lunch in the congressional dining room with Congressman Steve Bartlett from North Dallas (the district in which Prestonwood Baptist Church is located) and his wife. Congressman Bartlett apologized for insisting on lunch rather than dinner, which is the common practice in Washington.

"We have three children at home," he said, "and I try to eat with them as many nights of the week as possible." This congressman clearly had his priorities straight, which was just as significant as his 100-percent voting record for moral issues.

"How else do you reserve time for your family?" I asked him as we were eating together. He described a program similar to the one Bev and I adopted when I was the busy pastor of a growing church in San Diego.

At the first of each month he and his wife hold a calendar-planning session to schedule certain family days and evenings, six weeks to two months in advance. Then when someone asks to see him during these times, he can consult his calendar and honestly say, "I would love to go with you, but I have an appointment that night." Most parents who neglect quality times with their children do so because they have failed to prepare an adequate schedule, not because they do not love their children. Such planning is appropriate for both the twentieth and the 21st centuries.

5. Teach your children thrift, hard work, honesty, moral values, and personal responsibility.

These character principles are not intuitive; they must be taught. You cannot expect our secular schools to do this, and you will get little support from television. You and your church will be the primary communicators of these values, which are based on biblical authority. And your children need to see them exemplified in your life.

From the grammar school years on, youngsters should be paid an allowance for duties fulfilled around the home. Never "give" an allowance. Make it something they earn by doing the dishes or performing household chores. Issue clear guidelines and assignments, and then check up on your children to make sure they follow through. Teenagers do not automatically demonstrate responsibility in the work force when they find jobs; they must be trained by their parents. Young people who practice strong character principles will find employment in any era.

Today's parents face a problem that is more severe than ever before—peer pressure. For that reason increasing numbers of responsible parents are helping their teens select their friends. All parents should memorize one truism: "bad company corrupts good morals!" (1 Cor. 15:33, NAS).

Families have extraordinary tools, unavailable just forty years ago, to help them raise their children. A visit to one of over 6,000 Christian bookstores in the nation will acquaint you with the hundreds of helpful books on child rearing. While you are there, select cassette tapes of children's stories and beautiful music with which to fill your home, as well as video cassettes and many other aids to assist you in offsetting the harmful effects of a humanistically dominated culture. It is not enough to avoid secularism in your home. Give your family some positive alternatives by allowing your local Christian bookstore to supply them.

6. Develop the spiritual life of your family.

Individuals in every generation need to cultivate a strong spiritual life. That assignment is expressly given by God to the family and the church (Eph. 6:1–5; 4:11–16). You will neglect it to your peril.

From a practical standpoint, there are three minimum requirements for maintaining a growing spiritual life:

• Have daily family devotions.

Family worship is not a mystical religious ritual but a vital way to feed the spiritual needs of the family on a daily basis. Because of the pressures of modern living, fewer Christian families seem to be taking time each day to worship together. That is especially unfortunate because there are more helps for families today than ever before. I discovered this personally in 1984 when I was writing a short daily Bible study for over 20,000 supporters of my TV and radio ministry. Because of the expense involved, I polled these families to see if they were using this material. To my great disappointment, fewer than 700 indicated they wished to continue the Bible study for another year.

You need to establish daily devotions as a priority in your life. If you fail to recognize them as important for your family as daily food, it is unlikely that you will make time for them. Begin the tradition when the children are young and continue it through life. Devotions need not be long, perhaps ten minutes for Bible reading and five or ten minutes for prayer. Many children learn to pray at the family table. Such times of prayer should include 1) thanksgiving, 2) petition for others, and 3) requests for family and personal needs. This is also an ideal time for you to teach your children to pray for the missionary families of your church.

Two excellent family devotional programs have just been published: the Appleseed Series by Sheila Coleman for families with preschool children and _Together At Home_ by Dean and Grace Merrill for families with children six to twelve years old. I recommend that you look for them at your Christian bookstore.

For almost two thousand years Christian families have brought God into their children's lives on a daily basis through conducting family devotions. Many of today's Christian workers were reared in homes like this. No amount of 21st-century high-tech gadgetry will render the need for this practice obsolete. You will find it a worthy investment in raising your family.

• Teach your children to memorize Scripture.

As the secularization of society and the increase of information continues to multiply, it will become even more important for children to know God's Word by heart. The first psalm makes clear that the key to success is to have one's mentality rooted in the Word of God just as a tree's roots go down to the river for water.

Memorization can be a pleasurable experience for the entire family. Put your verses on cards and take them with you on trips, making a game out of reviewing learned verses. A child's mind is like a sponge; make sure your children soak up the right things. By learning one family verse a week, you will all commit to memory 500 Scripture verses in one decade. If they are the right verses, they will be sufficient to protect your child from the secularizing influences that surround him. For a list of 150 key verses to memorize, along with their titles, see my book *How to Study the Bible for Yourself.* And look for a series of picture books, the God's Word in My Heart series by Elspeth Murphy, which helps children to understand how a Bible verse applies to their lives and then to memorize it.

• Use your church as a spiritual friend to help you rear your children to love and serve God.

Our Lord said of His church, ". . . the gates of Hades shall not prevail against it" (Matt. 16:18). That promise extends into the 21st century. The church may be attacked and ridiculed, but it will continue to reach out in the next century to help families and individuals (more of that in the final chapter). The Bible-teaching church is the family's best friend, the one institution that inculcates the principles that your children so urgently need.

Your church also provides the proper environment for young people, formulating a peer group that shares your values. Today's active church offers something vital for every family member, which is why you must do everything possible to keep your children involved in the youth functions it sponsors.

Beware the Negative Power of Criticism. Never criticize your church at home. The negative effect on children when they hear parents criticize the pastor, the Sunday school teacher, or the youth director is devastating. Christian leaders make dreadful mistakes at times, but if you have aught against someone in your church, do what the Scripture says—go to him alone and discuss it. Then leave it to God. If you criticize church leaders openly, you limit their effectiveness at an important period in your children's lives. When you accompany your child to church, you want the pastor's message to reach the child's heart and mind to reinforce and supplement what you have been teaching at home. Adults may be able to disagree with the pastor and still receive a blessing from his message, but young people are not usually mature enough to make that transition.

When you have children of varying ages, maintaining an active role in a local church takes dedication. The process is both expensive and time consuming. But at the junior high and high school levels, you probably have no greater responsibility. I have found that parents who enjoy their adult children best later in life are those who sacrificed to ensure that the family used church activities to nurture and develop the children, particularly during the teenage years.

7. Put tight controls on your family's use of television.

Television is the most pervasive phenomenon of the last half of the twentieth century. Many consider it the enemy of family life not only because its programming represents an industry that is controlled by those hostile to traditional values but because it is a waste of time. Even its news features rarely provide in-depth coverage of significant issues.

As one communications professor notes, "Television is the command center of the culture!" He goes on to decree the fact that it teaches us so much surface information about so many things, few of which we can do anything about. This leads to "impotence," he explains, which may account for the very low involvement in civic affairs by the majority of the population. This professor laments that in the greatest country in the world, where one would expect over 90 percent of the population to get involved in the political process, only 59 percent participate in national elections.

Morally speaking, television has our culture by the throat. When women are projected as either nymphomaniacs or domineering shrews, TV is creating powerful and unnatural role models that will have a harmful effect on womanhood in the future. The fad in the 1985–86 season seems to be heroes and heroines of integrity and honor in all areas of life except morality. When the star of the program is Mister Clean in every way except his sexual promiscuity, he becomes a negative role model to millions of viewers. Your family does not need that kind of "education." In fact, Ephesians 5:1–10 makes it clear that the family cannot afford that kind of exposure.

Technology to the Rescue. Very likely before the end of this decade you will be able to purchase a small dish antenna for your home and have it beamed toward a signal controlled by individuals who share your moral values. For example, Dominion Satellite Network, which will enable the family to choose from three to six TV channels and up to five radio stations, should be operational within two years. This network is endorsed by twenty-four of the best known Christian programmers, so parents will never have to fear programming that shocks their moral sensibilities. As the mood of the country continues to move back toward traditional values, such wholesome programming will become increasingly popular and may even force the producers of some TV shows to clean up their scripts. In addition, such specialized TV networks can launch into

Figure 1

Television is the most powerful assault on the human mind ever invented. It is not good or bad in itself; that is determined by the moral values of those who control, write, and produce its programs. Current programing indicates that television is controlled by secular liberals, many of whom are hostile to religion and moral values. If television were controlled by those committed to Judeo-Christian ethics, it would be reflected in the program context.

educational programming that supplements both home school and regular school learning.

Always Evaluate the Source. Our Lord has taught us that "every good tree bears good fruit, but a bad tree bears bad fruit" (Matt. 7:17). Nowhere is this more obvious than in television programming and movies. Figure 1 graphically demonstrates that the philosophy of those who plan and produce the programming determines the moral values of what appears on television or film. Most programs today are produced in Hollywood or New York by individuals who consider moral values obsolete or, at best, meaningless. Some, of course, are so hostile to these traditional values that they use television to attack them. Though we may not be able to rectify that evil in the immediate future, we can create an alternative through Christian and traditional programming. Because of the enormous expense involved (about $1 billion to buy a network), even that will take a decade or so to accomplish.

Family TV Policy. What policy has your family established for the use of television? Most people have never sat down and laid out a strategy; consequently, they probably find themselves spending increased numbers of hours in front of the set. They also begin to make moral compromises as they view programs that reflect the declining standards of our day. This is particularly critical for families with teenagers, who are often subjected to programs that embarrass and humiliate them.

Whether parents realize it or not, they are then on trial before their own children. Do they possess the fortitude to shut off the set and refuse to be corrupted, or will they violate their consciences and continue to watch? We are "in the world" but are commanded not to be "of the world." When we allow the world to provide television viewing that violates our moral standards, we are subjecting ourselves to it.

Whenever I speak publicly on this subject, some father or mother volunteers that their family "got rid of the TV." These parents indicate that after three or four weeks of "withdrawal," family life was definitely enriched. Conversation expanded, reading habits improved, and the children's grades on tests improved. This is a step every Christian family should consider.

However, if you decide to keep your set, here are suggestions for regulating its use:

1. Establish TV viewing as a privilege, not a right; consequently, the owner of the set has the option to regulate and approve its use.

2. Only approved programs may be watched . . . news, sports, religious programs, public affairs, appropriate specials, and clean family programs (if you can find any).

3. Set time limits for viewing. One or two hours a night of even morally neutral programming can adversely affect children at certain grade levels. Television can be a great time waster.

4. Once a program has violated your moral values, scratch it off your list. That violation is an indication of the kinds of programs you can expect in the future.

5. Create alternatives to TV. After dinner, devotions, a game or two, a project, perhaps the evening news, homework, and bed time can complete any day's agenda.

The key to success is planning. If you don't control the television set, it will control you and your family.

8. Avoid unnecessary financial pressures.

The Christian cannot look to our "buy-now, pay-later" culture for financial guidance. Nor will our government serve as a model of fiscal responsibility, for it has already mortgaged the future of our children and grandchildren. The Word of God must be a Christian's financial counselor.

While the Bible admonishes us to trust God to take care of our needs in the future, it also teaches that He expects us to work hard, earn our own living, and pay our bills. In addition, He has promised to bless us financially if we honor Him by giving at least 10 percent of our income to His work in His name. For many Christian families, that includes paying Christian school or college tuition costs.

After knowing Christians from all economic levels of life, I have come to this conclusion: you will never have enough money to live on if you do not plan and follow a budget. Regardless of your income, it will not be enough without a solid financial program to make it work. (For information on budgeting, see my book *Spirit Controlled Family Living*.)

One little-understood key to financial success relates to the art of giving to God and then to others. Based on Luke 6:38, the more you give to God and to others in His name, the more He will give to you. John Wesley taught, "Give a tenth to God, save a tenth, and spend the rest." I would add, give something to the poor. In recent years Christians have tended to leave that responsibility to government. Unfortunately, government programs demand almost three dollars for the administration of every one dollar that really helps the poor. In addition, these programs often force the poor to seek the aid of government rather than God to supply their needs.

Sixty-five promises in the Bible indicate that God blesses those who befriend the destitute out of a pure heart. We are all facing an unsettled economic future. With bank failures, foreign debt, and balance of payment deficits so high that foreigners now own more of our money than we do, who can say that we will not experience a major 1929 economic crash before the turn of the century? Experts tell us that the stock market resembles the '29 pre-crash conditions. And while we can identify tangible signs of positive economic growth ahead, certain ominous signs suggest that we could experience a national financial disaster. If that happened in the United States, it would probably trigger a worldwide depression of unprecedented proportions.

I do not mean to be a prophet of gloom, for even if such a crash occurs, God will be there to help us in our time of trouble. But I would be less than faithful if I did not point out this possibility.

What Can We Do?

Such an event need not overtake us. In addition to honoring God with at least a tithe, giving generously to the poor, and living frugally within a planned budget, consider the following suggestions:

1. Avoid unnecessary debt. Pay cash whenever possible, and avoid interest costs, which are artificially high as a hedge against inflation. Some people pay for an item two or three times, depending on the interest rate charged for a loan.

2. Save something each payday. How you save is up to you, but many thoughtful people suggest that a portion of our savings should be held in hard money like silver and gold coins. Although they do not provide an interest rate of return, they are a hedge against the future. If an economic crash were to occur, those with

part of their savings in real money would possess spendable items to tide them over the difficult times. Remember, in such times of crisis, government tries to solve the problem by printing more paper money, drastically increasing the rate of inflation. I saw people in Germany after World War II paying a bushel basket full of German marks for a loaf of bread. Germans who possessed gold coins profited by inflation. In hyperinflation or a complete financial crash, gold or silver always has value.

Many believe that the economies of free world nations are so intertwined today that no country can afford to let the major banks in another major country go bankrupt, since all national economies would collapse like dominoes. Most people believe that the Federal Deposit Insurance Corporation (FDIC) would step in and pay up to $100,000 per depositor. Unfortunately, the largest banks in America carry more foreign loans than the FDIC has in its insurance fund. If these countries were unable to pay their debts, bank closings would exceed the government's ability to rectify the problem; a depression such as we have not known in fifty-five years would result.

In 1985 my new home-state of Virginia experienced extensive bank closures. When the state savings and loan companies became insolvent, hundreds of people could not withdraw their money. Long lines of depositors stood for days, trying to extract their hard-earned money out of a bankrupt institution. Finally the government had to declare a state of emergency.

One man I know, who had deposited his entire paycheck on Friday, could not gain access to his money on Monday. For weeks he could not pay his bills or even buy food. Can you imagine what would happen if banks closed all over the country? The best hedge against such an emergency is to possess something easy to carry, store, and hide, something that you can trade for food. Gold or silver coins fulfill those requirements.

By laying aside a few coins each month, you will gradually build up an emergency reserve, which will provide for you and your loved ones if such a scenario ever occurs. Such economic preparation will guarantee peace of mind. However, if you choose to buy silver or gold as part of your family's savings program, don't become paranoid or overly preoccupied with collecting material assets. Our trust is in the living God, not in silver or gold, and even economic emergencies do not change that. God, who has never failed His children in the past, will also be the God of the 21st century.

A reasonable financial program that makes ample provision for the Christian family's future includes 1) giving at least one-tenth to God; 2) saving one tenth (5 percent of which should be in currency or gold or silver coins during the first decade or so of marriage); 3) contributing something to the poor (local or world relief); and 4) carefully budgeting the rest while paying cash for all purchases except a home or car. This not only represents sound planning for the future, but also prevents financial pressure (one of the major causes of friction in marriage) from assailing your home.

9. Maintain a lifetime pattern of giving honor to both spouses' parents and, if necessary, be prepared to assume economic responsibility for them.

A serious deficiency of the Social Security program, begun just over a half century ago, is that it shifts responsibility for the elderly away from the family to the government; therefore, many senior citizens are neglected by their children.

Senior Citizens and the Family. After fifty years of the Social Security program, almost everyone admits it is in trouble. Rates, which have gone out of sight, are now referred to as taxes. The drastic drop in the size of families lowers the number of those contributing to the fund which makes it unlikely that young people starting out in the program will ever collect any benefits unless the government subsidizes it, and politics being what they are, this is a real possibility.

None of the Social Security experts anticipated that medical science would be so successful in extending life spans for both men and women. The average male in this country is expected to reach seventy-four years of age; the average woman, seventy-nine. Our seventy-five-year-old president, who expects to finish his administration at seventy-nine, and five Supreme Court justices, who are older than the president and do not show intentions of resigning, inspire most of us to anticipate outliving this average life expectancy. As exciting a prospect as this is to those of us who already show extensive mileage on our speedometers, it is devastating to Social Security, which was designed for people with shorter life spans.

As a citizen observer of the entire life of this fifty-year-old system, I find its worst trait is its influence upon the biblical teaching of caring for relatives who are elderly. Before Social Security reared its ugly head with false promises, Mom and Dad were cared for by their children. Admittedly, living conditions became crowded and certain disadvantages arose, but the emotional support for the elderly and the example of children "honoring their parents" was a testimony to grandchildren. In addition, the extended family had a positive influence on the home. Today many children grow up without knowing their grandparents, often because the elderly have been shuttled off to homes to be cared for by the government. Senior citizens are not going to disappear. In fact, their numbers will expand in the years ahead. The church of Jesus Christ has a golden opportunity to set an example by treating them as an integral part of the family, with dignity, love, and respect, rather than as unnecessary baggage. We should start by genuinely reassuring our parents of our love and letting them know that we will never forsake them. Whether such a pledge is ever used by them or not, it is emotionally beneficial for older people to know that they will always have a place to live and someone who always will care for them lovingly. The potential loss of Social Security benefits will not worry the senior citizen who is confident of that. Such assurance may well contribute to the health, well-being, and longer life of the parents, which, according to Ephesians 6:1–3, will lengthen the lives of their children.

10. Use your home for hospitality evangelism.

Some things never change! One of them is the Great Commission, which is appropriate for any century. In Matthew 28:18–20 our Lord gave us the command, through His disciples, to preach the gospel with His help "even to the end of the age." If He does not come before the 21st century, we will still have the privilege of leading individuals to the Savior. Millions of Christians share their faith regularly, which is doubtlessly one of the reasons so many people are coming to Christ in our generation.

The high-tech age, as Naisbitt points out, has produced a hunger in the hearts of millions for "high-touch"—his term for human contact. Society is so impersonal today that millions go through life lonely, afraid, and desperately seeking companionship. Christians should increasingly be on the alert to befriend those who need the Savior. Your home Bible study (weekly or monthly) offers a warm, friendly atmosphere for your neighbors to be introduced to the Lord.

The first step is to put your home on the altar and dedicate it to Him as a vehicle to lead others to Christ. The early church "went from house to house" teaching the word. Like them, you have something to offer your neighbors that they cannot get anywhere else—the Word of God. Your home is the ideal place for such an outreach program.

The family has always been the basis of society, and it will continue to be, not only in the next century but as long as the human race exists. The best way to prepare your family for the future is to incorporate God's principles into your family life today.

11

How Can the Church Utilize This Golden Opportunity?

I'M bullish on the future role of the church of Jesus Christ in the 21st century. For if the church continues growing at the rate it has during the past fifty years—and a good case can be made that it will accelerate that growth rate—most Americans will profess a born-again experience with Jesus Christ (51–52 percent of the population by the year 2000 at the present rate reflected in the Gallup Poll). And if the church continues to become involved politically during the next decade at the rate it has for the past ten years, we will have the same representation in government that we have in the population. Such a welcome change in the philosophy of the local, state, and national legislators, judges, and government bureaucrats would set humanism's influence on our culture back fifty years where it belongs and produce a morally sane and safe society.

One important factor that futurists like Toffler and Naisbitt have missed is that Christian involvement in civic affairs is growing in two ways at the same time. Liberalism, on the other hand, is dying. Every election finds fewer liberals calling enough people even to go out and vote. Through evangelism, more conservative voters are created (even converted campus radicals turn conservative 70 to 80 percent of the time because of faithful Bible teaching) by the time election day rolls around every two years. Add to that the fact that more noninvolved Christians (many who formerly were not even registered to vote) are recruited to the Conservative Megatrend every two years. No wonder the _Washington Post_ published an article in mid-1986 entitled "The Christians Are Coming!" They really are—and the next decade will prove it.

Another reason I am bullish on the future of the church is that our Lord promised, "I will build My church, and the gates of Hades shall not prevail against it" (Matt. 16:18). We can be assured that the church will endure to the end of the age, whenever that occurs. We also have the promise that many will accept Christ as Savior in the end times so that "a great multitude . . . of all nations, tribes, peoples, and tongues" (Rev. 7:9) will stand before the Lord and worship Him.

New technology may help the church fulfill this prophecy. We could be on the verge of witnessing the greatest soul harvest in the history of man. Before dismissing me as a super-optimist, examine my five reasons for believing this. Then look with me at some of the changes the church might make to meet this challenge.

The High-Tech Explosion in Information

Before the end of this century, technology may become the hand-maiden of the church. If believers are progressive enough to utilize the technology of new telecommunications, we will be able to reach many more souls with the message of the gospel. One fact never changes; men and women cannot be saved until they "hear" the gospel. Both our Lord (in Matt. 13) and the apostle Paul (in Rom. 10: 8–17) emphasized that. Twenty-first century technology will open new opportunities to communicate to every human being in the world.

Audio and Visual Advancements

Just imagine what voice-activated computers could do for the evangelist who only knows one language. He will be able to preach in his mother tongue, and his words will be processed by the computer into the language of another tribe or nation. Already computers have shortened the time it takes Bible translators to reproduce the Scriptures in the tongue of a tribe. Think what it will mean when an evangelist can communicate directly with these people in their native language. Miniaturization leads to portability so that such devices may some day become accessible to the most remote areas. But technology will not only come to our aid in primitive areas. Now that the electric church of radio and television is becoming acceptable to the church, we should see a new wave of use for it.

I can visualize the day when television sets are hooked to telephone lines that enable a person to call his church's video library and take Bible study training in his home. I recently did a series of premarital counseling sessions for a video company to market to churches across the country, which will save busy pastors from having to share such lessons repeatedly with each prospective couple. In the future, couples won't even have to drive to the church; such training can be offered in their homes. The same kind of training could be utilized as a follow-up to pastoral marriage counseling. I would not be surprised to see Christian colleges directing video curricula from the campus straight into the home. This way college costs would conform to everyone's budget.

I have already mentioned the Dominion Satellite Network, which will provide six cable channels controlled by Christians. I know of two new conservative groups that are planning to launch cable TV networks in the near future. The three original charismatic networks—CBN, TBN, and PTL—will doubtless expand greatly in the future as 80 percent of American homes are wired for cable and other aggressive thinkers will develop new ones.

The first fundamentalist, noncharismatic cable network in the country was established early in 1986 when Jerry Falwell bought the Christian Cable Network (CCN) and a satellite capability. The Southern Baptists may also expand their ACTS network someday to reach millions of homes in the country. Still other homes will probably be accessible by direct broadcast antennae, rather than cable.

Churches Using Computers

For several years now aggressive churches have made peace with computers. In fact, I recently asked the business manager of a church where I was preaching if their staff owned a computer. He responded, "Yes, we have three of them."

Almost any church can afford a computer or find a businessman in the congregation who will donate one. Space does not permit me to describe all that computers can do for churches, such as personalized mailings, attendance record-keeping, personalized birthday and anniversary cards, and giving and stewardship records.

Although some members may fear that computers will make the church less personal, just the opposite can result from careful planning. The pastor can remember the birthday of each parishioner with a card, letter, or phone call. Members can be notified of new parishioners in their area so that they can get acquainted and offer Christian hospitality. The computer can identify absentees, and then these persons can be contacted by a note or personal visit. If I were pastoring today, I would try to establish a computer high-tech chairman to bring all the experienced people in the congregation together and discuss how computers could best be used to enhance the church's ministry. One wave of the future, as we shall see, should be to provide vocational training and retraining of those automated out of a profession.

Churches need to lead the way in this field. We have the facilities, the personnel, and the compassion for what will be a major need in most communities.

The Death and Emptiness of Enlightenment Humanism

Victims of the philosophy of secular humanism are turning elsewhere for answers to their questions about life, death, and eternity, which is opening up to the gospel some people who earlier in life had rejected its premises. Skepticism may seem appealing to a youth who expects sixty more years of life, but it is difficult to be an old atheist. Even Voltaire cried out for mercy on his death bed. More recently, it is rumored that Jean Paul Sartre, the French humanist existentialist, called upon God during his dying hours.

I do not fault these men or try to demean them for invoking God's mercy as they stood on the brink of eternity. That is a normal response to impending death, known in the Bible as "the fear of death," since it is frightening to contemplate an uncertain future and an ultimate meeting with God—an intuitive certainty that seems written by Him on the human heart.

Other cases could be cited to illustrate the point that millions who recognize the futility of human wisdom, whether it be secular humanism or a self-styled rejection of God, are realizing that man does not have the answers that count. Consequently, the church and its people have a golden opportunity to point these empty souls to the truth found in Jesus Christ.

The Basic Respect of American People for Christ and His Church

Despite fifty years of incessant attack by humanists on religion, the majority of our citizens have continued to respect the church, the Bible, and ministers. Humanists have fired their best guns, but they are gradually losing the battle.

The fifty-year study *Religion in America* by the Gallup Organization, released in May of 1985, indicates that "seven in 10 U.S. adults say they are members of a church or synagogue." It further states that "4 in 10 adults attend church in a typical week." "Seven in 10 Americans (72 percent) believe the Bible to be the word of God while only 23 percent hold that it is not." According to the report, "95% of Americans believe in God," (as a "unifying and organizing power behind the universe"), and 66 percent of these "believe in a personal God who watches over and judges people—the God of Biblical revelation to whom man is answerable."[1]

Regarding the very important subject of a person's belief in Jesus Christ as God, which is essential to salvation (Acts 4:12), Gallup's 1985 report offers some interesting statistics. "Seventy percent believe Jesus is God"; eight in ten believe "that Jesus was divine . . . at least in some respects. . . . 6 in 10 indicate they are strongly convinced of his divinity. Similarly, 8 in 10 say that they believe Jesus rose from the dead (physically or spiritually), but closer to 6 in 10 express the certainty that he did so."[2]

One particular aspect of these statistics should inspire Christians and churches: 20 percent more believe in the deity and resurrection of our Lord than profess a born-again experience. These individuals do not need to be convinced of His deity; they simply need to see that they are lost unless they personally accept Christ. Many of them have probably never been taught that they must be "born again" (John 3:3–4). That translates into 47 million unsaved believers in Christ's deity who should be apt subjects for personal salvation. I hope you, as a reader of this book, will let God use your life to lead some of those 47 million to Himself. Some live in your neighborhood, and you probably work with others. Or you may need to receive Christ into your life by prayerfully inviting Him to forgive your sin and to become your Lord and Savior.

Christians' Increased Boldness in Sharing Their Faith

The book of Acts indicates that the early church members "went from house to house" sharing the gospel. Excuses, such as "sophisticated people don't talk to others about their religion," are giving place to a realization that people desperately need Christ. A nurse told me recently that she led her first soul to Christ—an AIDS victim. She confessed that she had always been too timid to share her faith, but this dying soul's plight forced her to begin a conversation that resulted in his salvation.

As we have already seen, the Gallup Poll indicates that 5 million Christians, or 1 in 12, share their faith every week. In addition, 25 million, or 1 out of every 2.5 Christians, has shared his faith at least once. This should increase in the future as new Christians attend some of the many personal evangelism training programs, resulting in an enormous number of individuals turning to Christ. Can you imagine what would happen if we doubled those figures during the next fourteen years?

Such a soul harvest would not only provide a second chance for those who may have lived a hedonistic lifestyle during their teens and twenties but should also bring many individuals in the pro-life and conservative movements to personal faith in Christ. Many of these concerned patriots were turned off by religion in their early lives because if the theological bickering among denominations. Now that Christians are learning to respect and appreciate each other without sacrificing their theological differences, these people are more open to our message. Besides, as they get older, they realize that their moral values are really rooted in religious faith.

The Ministry of the Holy Spirit

Our Lord taught that the Holy Spirit was like the wind that blows where it wills; though we "hear the sound," we don't know where it goes or where it comes from (John 3:8). It seems to me that the moving of the Holy Spirit has been increasing in velocity during the past twenty years. The "Spirit-filled life" almost seemed like a heretical expression to the fundamental church just twenty years ago. Many who felt uncomfortable with such expressions then have now adopted not only the language but the daily experience. Whole denominations that twenty years ago rarely mentioned the Spirit's special ministry in the church, today talk freely about His power, His leading, and His blessing. I know of no group that is unaware that He is indispensable to His church and to the believer. And since "the Word of truth," the Bible, has been translated into so many versions, we may anticipate a fresh new wave of the Spirit's ministry.

Anyone familiar with the work of the Holy Spirit in South America, Africa, and other places in the world will testify that God is doing something special in this day—and His work is increasing. As we approach the end of this millennium, we can expect an increase in the effective ministry of the Holy Spirit—which will likely result in an increased soul harvest.

Second Millennium Hysteria

For the second time since our Lord's ascension into heaven, we are about to close out a thousand-year period. The last decade of the first millennium found a number of individuals and groups proclaiming that the event would be accompanied by some cataclysmic occurrence in the heavens. It was not uncommon for some to predict the end of the age by the year 1000. We identify that period as "The Dark Ages," a time when the Bible was kept from the people. Even if they had had access to a Bible, few of the common people could read. Today we have more Bibles than people, so we should approach the year 2000 with a better understanding of God's ways.

I look for the revival of the old chiliast theory of our Lord's return, the thousand-year-one-day theory, which maintained that our Lord would usher in His age of peace in the 21st century. This theory, which dates back to the second and third centuries A.D., suggested that the six days of creation would be duplicated in God's plan of the ages. The 4,000 years before Christ (B.C.) and the 2,000 years after Christ (A.D.) signify a total of 6 days; these 6,000 years would be followed by the millennial age of Christ's rule on earth or the Sabbath of Rest. Therefore, the year 2000 or the 21st century would end the world as we now know it and usher in the millennium or the age of peace.

I am not advocating this theory—just predicting it will probably make a popular comeback. Bible-believing Christians realize that the Lord will come "at an hour you do not expect" (Luke 12:40); they know that no man knows the day or the hour when our Lord will return (see Matt. 24:36). Still the revival of this theory is likely to create a new wave of insecurity about the future, which will afford the church a golden opportunity to win souls to Christ. A person who is secure in a personal relationship to Christ knows that the end of this age is just the beginning of heavenlike conditions here on earth.

I look for a new interest in Bible prophecy to develop in the very near future and continue into the next century. Such a fascination with the future will naturally lead to renewed Bible study focusing largely on the Book of Revelation, since it provides more definitive details on the future than any other book. As people search the Scriptures regarding the future, many will come to faith.

New Methods for a 2,000-Year-Old Church

These five trends and the explosion of technology and telecommunications lead me to believe that the next decade provides a phenomenal opportunity for the church to preach the gospel. This could provide the greatest period of church growth in American history. Let me suggest nine ways the church can prepare to meet this challenge. These suggestions are based on my thirty years experience as the pastor of growing churches and my research into the impact of technology on the church of the future. Bible-teaching, Spirit-filled, soul-winning churches that incorporate these nine characteristics cannot help but grow as they minister to the needs of the people.

1. Meet the increasing need for love, warmth, and caring.

We have already noted that one of Naisbitt's major megatrends included the need for "high-touch" in our high-tech society. If that is true today, we can only imagine how impersonal life in the next century will be as technology engulfs the work place, isolating people from each other in the process. When such individuals go to church, they will reflect an increasing need to be with people.

Many of our newer, more progressive churches have designed conversation centers near the sanctuary for people to fellowship with one another before or after church. It was once thought blasphemous to serve coffee before an adult Bible study. Today an increasing number of churches do it—not because the people need the coffee but because the social situation breaks down their reserve and promotes conversation. I watched this happen to my large class, which gathers each Sunday in the 4,000-seat auditorium of the Prestonwood Baptist Church. For the first few weeks the class was composed of 500 individuals scattered all over the auditorium. After one of the women volunteered to serve coffee and donuts before class, I saw people coming together to talk, make acquaintances, and build friendships.

The more impersonal society becomes, the more we should strive for closeness when individuals enter the church, thus fulfilling a basic human need. Some pastors even incorporate this appropriately into the church service. Many congregations of very sophisticated people, like those at Prestonwood, are given an opportunity during the morning service to shake hands and introduce themselves to four or five others.

Pastor Glen Cole and His Caring Church. One of the most beautiful illustrations of church fellowship occurred the second Sunday after my friend Pastor Glen Cole of the Church in Sacramento and his congregation had opened their new 3,000-seat church. He had invited me to preach at both morning services that day, and I watched him lead his congregation in worship and praise. Then he led them in the offering. After the solo the ushers came to the front to dedicate the tithes and offerings.

Coming halfway down the platform steps, Pastor Cole asked how many people needed prayer to help them find work or change vocations. Over twenty hands went up in each service. He then invited someone standing near each person to step over and, as a point of contact, put a hand on them. Very quietly, members of the church did so. As a young man in his mid-twenties, with his wife and child, indicated he was out of work, a well-dressed businessman in his fifties stepped over, put his hand on the young father's shoulder, and stood silently as the pastor offered a moving prayer.

When this young man sat down, I saw a look of joy in his face as he thought, *Here is a church that cares!* After the benediction the businessman walked out of church, chatting with the young man in need of a job. When I told Pastor Cole about this incident, he said that he prays for those out of work regularly, and God has performed many miracles as their members help others in the congregation find work.

You may never have seen anything like this before and may even deem it inappropriate for a morning worship service. But it isn't. This pastor of a large congregation has discovered a way to help the body of Christ minister to its hurting members. This kind of warmth and care will be increasingly necessary in the years ahead as we continue to minister to people.

2. Provide vocational guidance and assistance.

We have already noted that millions of people between now and the 21st century will probably be automated out of a profession as we progress from an industrial society into the information age. This will undoubtedly impact the church as millions of Christians seek entirely new professions.

The church must take advantage of this golden opportunity to pool its resources, provide training classes, offer vocational counseling and testing, and even institute job placement programs. We need to train our people to keep on the alert for vocational opportunities where they work and call them in to the career guidance secretary, who will put the information into the computer and screen available candidates. Many congregations have people qualified to implement such a program; all they need is someone to lead it. Someday large churches will probably add a vocational guidance pastor or director to the staff. A robust vocational program will be difficult for small churches, so large churches should invite them to participate in searching for vocational opportunities as well as referring individuals for job placement.

I may be criticized for such a suggestion today, but by the mid-nineties I expect to find cities with more than one progressive church implementing such a program. After all, churches offer seminars and training sessions on family life and marriage, time and money management, and personal soul winning. Why not vocational guidance and placement? Even a few classes on how to apply for a job would be helpful. A dedicated deacon in my Bible class has hired over 500 people during his career. Surely some sessions by such a brother would be helpful for young people looking for work. Remember, too, if a person has worked in one place for twenty-five years, he probably knows very little about applying for a new job.★

The church of the future will have to be interested in the whole person and the family. A progressive Canadian pastor in Toronto showed me a creative pre- and postnatal care program his church sponsored for the entire community, attracting a large population of young married couples. We have focused upon the spiritual part of the parishioner and remanded the educational process to the public sector of education for too long. Because that sector is controlled largely by secular humanists, who are doing a dreadfully poor job of teaching even the basics, the church should step into the gap and help people in every area of their lives. The church of the future should, next to the family, be the center of our activities. A church

★For information regarding Dr. LaHaye's Temperament Test to help you analyze your basic talents and capabilities, including fifty suggestions of appropriate vocations for your temperament, see p. 213.

that fulfills this role faithfully will never lack for members during any century.

3. Provide Bible-based preaching with practical life application.

Ever since the Fall of man in the Garden of Eden, man's life has been filled with problems, and this will not change in the next century. Therefore, God gave us the Bible to understand the mysteries of life, God, and the future. There will always be a need for Bible teaching—as long as it includes practical application.

The church must resist all temptations to modernize its message as it adapts its methods to new technological changes. Most churches that are true to the Word of God agree essentially on certain basic doctrines:

- the inspiration and inerrancy of the Word of God;
- the Triune Godhead;
- the unique deity of our Lord Jesus Christ;
- the ministry of the Holy Spirit;
- the offer of salvation by grace through faith;
- the need to disciple the saints through the study of the Word of God;
- the challenge of holy living;
- and the command of our Lord and His apostles to evangelize the lost of the world.

These basic hallmarks of Christianity seem characteristic of the growing churches of our day. Preachers of all denominations who emphasize these truths and apply them to the daily lives of their congregations are preaching to ever increasing numbers. Liberal ministers are continually complaining of diminishing numbers. Liberalism, which deals fast and loose with God's Word and sound doctrine, has no message for today, and the vanishing liberal congregations reflect this fact.

Historically man (including ministers) has often been tempted to modify God's Word to his own will. Cain, for instance, presented a vegetable offering, which offended God, instead of the animal sacrifice that the Lord commanded. The church must follow the example of Cain's brother, Abel, who sacrificed an animal just as God commanded him.

Like Cain, many church leaders have tried to introduce either their own ideas or those that would appeal more strongly to the people of their day. The Bible forbids this! In fact, the last chapter of the Bible pronounces a curse on anyone who adds to or subtracts from the words written in God's book.

The church endured its greatest times of failure when it stopped preaching the Word and was overrun by a pagan or humanistic culture. During these periods of apostasy the church tampered with doctrine and taught the traditions of men instead of the Word of God.

The church of the 21st century must avoid this error or it, too, will fail. God can use the church to save people and to improve the moral climate of its culture only when Christians have a deep commitment to the truths of Scripture. The early church (the church of the first three centuries), the Reformation church, the missionary churches of the eighteenth century, and the current Bible-believing churches all had powerful influences on their cultures because they preached the truth.

Theological preaching alone, however, does not build churches and change lives. As I look at the booming churches across the land, I see that most of the pastors faithfully teach the Word of God *and* apply it to the lives of the people. Such preachers will be in even greater demand in the future.

4. We must improve our ministry to the family.

The church must be more aware of the four family structures that exist today and will exist in the future. For years we have based our ministry to families solely on the traditional family, which we often saw as a father, a wife who did not work outside the home, and one or more children.

That approach is woefully out of date. Today wives in over 45 million families work outside the home. Therefore, the church must reappraise its ministry to this majority of families with two working parents. In days gone by, Dad sat down to a hot meal that was ready the moment he arrived home so the family could attend a myriad of week-night church activities. Churches could sustain good attendance at midweek prayer services, evangelistic outreach or calling meetings, men's and women's groups, and choir practice. Today, even though the church is growing, it is not always possible to expect a participatory level equal to that of thirty years ago. A pastor should not make members of these modern families feel guilty if they are not able to attend every weeknight activity conducted by the church.

Second, we must admit that the burgeoning number of single-parent families in this country is all but ignored by many churches. As I travel the country holding Family Life Seminars in large churches, I find a growing discontent—and in many cases anger—from this needy group of believers.

Often they protest, "My church ignores me." "Mine has nothing for me. The entire ministry seems to be directed only to traditional families. Why can't we be considered real people?" One individual observed, "My church led me to Christ, baptized me, and accepts my tithe, but it will not forget my divorce." Another divorcée remarked, "Ex-criminals, former prostitutes, and all non-Christians are received with open arms. Divorced people are treated like lepers."

In an attempt to stem the tide of permissiveness, we fundamentalists often thunder against immorality and divorce—and well we should. But our condemnation needs to be balanced with love and forgiveness for those who have sinned and are forgiven by God.

Some pastors are easily offended when the members of the church do not measure up to their ideals. To me the church is like a service station designed by God to pump up the downhearted, repair the broken, rebuild the crippled, and re-energize the dead. Pastors are obligated to accept people as they are and lovingly teach them God's blueprint for their lives. We must be like the prodigal son's father who ran to meet his sinful son and kissed him. The undeserving boy had done nothing more than leave the pigpen to return to his comfortable home. Remember, the only people Jesus indicted during His ministry were unrepentant rebels.

Have you ever put yourself in the shoes of the man or woman who was saved after divorce? Consider, for instance, the twenty-eight-year-old divorced mother of three, who at eighteen made the dreadful mistake of marrying her unsaved boyfriend. Everything in our family-oriented church and life-style reminds her that the best she can do in life represents the secondary or circumstantial will of God, not His perfect will.

Or what about the unwed mother who, in an unguarded moment of passion, exchanged her virtue for the weight of a life-style with her fatherless child? She has enough heartache! If her God could forgive the woman taken in adultery, the murderous Saul of Tarsus, and the Peter who denied Him, does He not hear her cries of repentance?

Of course! you say. But can your church equal His divine forgiveness? Does it treat her as an outcast? Or does the church reach out to her in love?

I have often been intrigued by the fact that many fundamentalist ministers use a Scofield Reference Bible for preaching. Most don't realize it was compiled by a divorced lawyer—C.I. Scofield. Obviously God can use divorced people. Hopefully the church of the future will find a place for these people to serve their Lord.

Widows also need the support of their churches. Having been reared by a widowed mother with three small children, I must confess that our fundamentalist church seldom supplied our needs. A few (bless their hearts) tried. Some of the men occasionally offered to repair my mother's car or do some "fixin' around the house," but most of the time she faced her problems alone.

Admittedly, difficulties arise when Christians administer love and support, but the church should be an example of love to God's sheep as well as a gospel lighthouse. Hopefully, we will see an increasing emphasis on ministry to this large group in our churches as we approach the late eighties and nineties. Do not make them wait until they die and go to heaven to feel like first-class citizens in the family of God. Assigning a deacon and his wife to each single-parent family to call on, advise, and help them, and even to serve as foster grandparents to the children would be an appropriate start.

One of the basic needs of the single parent (male or female) is fellowship. Singles are often neglected by even the most hospitable church entertainers, a lesson I learned from my mother. She urged her married friends to include at least two singles in after-church hospitality. That way "the single doesn't feel like a fifth wheel."

Finally, the church needs to re-evaluate its ministry to the single-person household, which is the fourth family structure of today and the future. Our churches need to find unique leaders to work with the wide variety of persons who live alone and who are a major portion of the harvest our Lord entrusted to us.

Actually, such a ministry costs the church nothing in the long run. After the first year a singles pastor will have drawn more than enough singles to his church to cover all that department's expenses. Singles are one of the most financially independent groups in the church, often possessing more discretionary money than any other group. They are also more apt to yield themselves to the Lord for Christian service than other groups because their lives are less complicated. Instead of making them feel uncomfortable in our "traditional" churches, we need to include singles in the life line of the congregation. Unless a special department is dedicated to them, it is doubtful this can happen.

5. Improve our ministry to the poor.

Every day it becomes more apparent that government aid to the poor is inefficient, costly, and, in some cases, harmful to the family. In addition, at its present rate of growth, it could collapse under its own weight. A recent report estimates that in 1985, local, state, and federal costs of welfare, Social Security, and Medicare/Medicaid have exceeded $600 billion. And these are good times! The jobless rate is below 7 percent, the economy is thriving, and people are optimistic about the future; yet we are spending ourselves into bankruptcy on government handouts.

Twenty years ago some felt that government could take the place of God in supplying man's basic needs. Today we know better. Unlike God, government is distinctly limited in its resources. Just imagine what it would be like if we entered a recession or deep depression and the jobless rate skyrocketed to 15 or 20 percent, as it could before the next century.

The churches of the land need to rethink their attitude toward social concern and begin programs for the poor. During the thirties and forties, the fundamental branch of Christianity seemed to swing so far away from the liberal's practice of social involvement that we have gained the reputation of being cold and unconcerned about the poor. When liberals left the faith, shifting from evangelistic concern for the lost to social concern for the poor, they gained acceptance with the media and humanists in academia because their message was not offensive to atheism and they all shared common concerns for the needy.

We in the Bible-believing church need to evaluate our Lord's teaching about the poor. Instead of entrusting the social needs of the poor in our congregations to the government, we should assume a responsibility to reach out and help them. God has always promised special blessings to those who assist the destitute. It is not enough for churches to send $50 a month to a local rescue mission. We need to develop programs that will encourage us to give of our means and of ourselves.

6. Develop better programs for ministering to the elderly.

Modern medical science and improved living conditions have doubled the life expectancy of our citizens. That longevity could be increased another 20 percent by the 21st century. In the year 2000 the average man may live to be eighty-five, the average woman over ninety. That will not only destroy the present Social Security system but increase the number of seniors in our churches, giving them many additional years to serve their Lord. These active seniors would be excellent prospects to direct the vocational and help-the-poor programs mentioned above. Everyone needs to be needed, and that is even more true of senior citizens.

7. Emphasize holy living.

The principles of God never change. A central spiritual principle, that of holy living, is particularly essential because we live in the most sexually surcharged day in the history of man. All citizens are constantly bombarded by sexual temptation. Unless we experience a supernatural miracle of revival before the end of the nineties, I doubt that things will be different in the first part of the 21st century.

For that reason the church, ever the conscience of God to His people as well as to the world about them, should clearly set forth His standard for holy living. Adultery, fornication, homosexuality, dishonesty, and other sins of man are still condemned by the Holy Scriptures. If the church's voice on these subjects is stilled, who will convey the message? The public schools, government, or media?

None of these will until more Christians and other religious individuals who share our values take up positions in these important arenas.

The need for such teaching is obvious to anyone who has eyes to see. In early 1986 a Roper Poll indicated that 61 percent of the adult population thought it was permissible for unmarried teens to engage in premarital sex—almost double the 1969 figure (32 percent).[3] Obviously the voice of the church has been either silenced or obscured by the voices of the media and sex educators.

Time magazine reported that 1 million unwed teenage girls will get pregnant this year, 30,000 of them under 15 years of age. According to present trends, "40% of today's 14-year-old girls will be pregnant at least once before the age 20."[4] Are we not in desperate need of moral and spiritual revival?

Many of those pregnant girls will be visitors or members in our churches during their teen years. They need to hear pastors, youth pastors, and leaders emphasize the timeless moral standards of God to help offset the many modern voices enticing them to permissiveness.

The church must also emphasize God's unchanging standard for lifetime marriages even though we need to be loving and helpful to the victims of divorce. As I travel across the country I encounter an alarming increase of divorce among long-time Christians. Instead of letting their real or imagined problems in marriage drive them to the church for help in reconciliation, Christians often seek counsel from humanists whose advice counters that of the Word of God. Psalm 1:1 warns the child of God not to walk in the counsel of the ungodly. We adopt worldly philosophies and standards in our personal and family lives at our peril. The church needs to emphasize that fact in an attempt to bring our people and our culture back into conformity with God's Word.

8. Become more politically involved and active.

Politics need not be a dirty business! As a necessary part of life and God's well-established plan for man, it should attract the involvement of many more church members.

We have already seen that our numbers in the population and our commitment to biblical and traditional values confront the church with the opportunity to change the future through the electoral process. By increasing our involvement in future elections, we can supply government with moral and qualified candidates for public office. By registering all our members, by educating them concerning both the moral issues of the day and the voting records of the candidates, and by encouraging our people to vote, we can make the difference in future elections.

This does not mean that we should neglect soul winning or church building while we wrest control of government from humanists and liberals through the electoral process. As we saw in chapter six, many of the greatest soul winners in the nation have become increasingly active in the political process. They realize that if the secularizers are not defeated at the polls soon, they will use the awesome power of government to curtail religious freedom in this country—and our opportunities to win souls will similarly be lessened.

Everything in Moderation. Most of us will not sustain a high level of interest in politics for more than three- or four-months every two years, because, as Christians, we are primarily motivated by our concern for the Kingdom of God. But it is not necessary for us to be active politically on a continual basis in order to be effective. Due to our large numbers in the population, a three or four month commitment during election years is sufficient to have a significant influence on who wins or loses elections. In months prior to a local or national election, Christians should offer their services to a candidate who shares their values and help him or her get elected. Part-time volunteer work at such crucial times can provide many years of good government after their candidate is elected.

In 1986 a thirty-five-year-old Baptist minister, Joe Lutz, filed to run for the U.S. Senate in Oregon against a long-term popular incumbent. Seriously limited by less money than his opponent, Lutz polled 44 percent of the vote. What was his secret? Seven thousand campaign volunteers! He recruited and trained 7,000, mostly Christians, to campaign on his behalf.

In many congressional districts 500 such volunteers could cause an upset. Campaign workers are often worth more to a candidate than money.

Another thing Christians can do is offer to serve on their church's good government committee or begin such a committee if their church does not have one. They can also volunteer to serve on a "get-out-the-vote" telephone committee, which organizes a campaign to call every registered member of the congregation on election day to make sure they go to the polls for your church. Such a campaign by two hundred or more churches can make the difference in close elections.

Some Christians, when led by the Spirit of God, need to prayerfully consider running for public office themselves. This group can change the future of this country through legislative reform.

Vigorously Oppose Ungodliness. Silence is not always golden! Sometimes our silence is cowardice. At best it is interpreted as approval. For more than twenty years since the Supreme Court legalized the immoral publication of pornography, Christians and other religious people kept silent while the porn trade grew to an annual $8 billion business. Less than 37 percent of the nation ever bought porn, according to a *Newsweek* magazine report, but the majority remained silent as the leading sellers of that mental corruption printed millions of copies.[5]

Gradually that has changed. Christians and other concerned citizens have raised their voices in protest, staged peaceful demonstrations, rallies, and pickets, and, finally, led boycotts of stores selling pornography. In 1985 and 1986 over 10,000 stores discontinued the sale of objectionable material resulting in great financial injury to these industries. Even as I write this chapter I have heard the announcement that *Playgirl* has declared bankruptcy and *Playboy* has lost over a million dollars in the first half of the year.

In spite of the opposition of our liberal press, we are finally getting our message to the American people that pornography is a moral blight on any society. It produces violent rape, child molestation, incest, and sexual promiscuity, and the best defense against it is to make it illegal. Since, however, our liberal Supreme Court and Congress refuse to do that, the citizens of the nation must use their freedom to be selective where they shop in order to shut down the sources selling this harmful material.

This should be of particular concern to Christians who are taught to be good stewards of their treasure. It is not enough to tithe 10 percent of our income. We should be selective about where we spend the other 90 percent. Very few business firms can afford to alienate the 40 percent of their potential customers who are born-again and may decide not to shop in stores that traffic in pornography.

9. Pray for your government and future government leaders.

First Timothy 2:1–5 commands us to pray for those in authority over us. Christians should pray for the president, the justices of the Supreme Court, and all elected officials within their congressional districts—school board members, county supervisors, city council members, sheriffs, and state and U.S. senators and representatives (for a free chart to use in praying for national officials, write ACTV, 122 "C" St. NW, Suite 850, Washington, D.C., 20001).

As Christians begin praying for government officials, we can expect God to work in the hearts of many currently in office and to replace those who make legislative decisions based on humanism with legislators who will make those important decisions based on the Judeo-Christian values that originally characterized this nation.

The Purpose of Government. There seems to be a good deal of confusion about the real purpose of government. Even Christians who pray for government officials according to 1 Timothy 2:1–5 don't seem to realize that God intended government to conduct its affairs so its citizens could: 1) lead a quiet life, and 2) lead a peaceable life in godliness (moral decency) and in reverence. The eighteenth and nineteenth centuries, characterized by these conditions as "nation under God," were both morally sane and socially safe. That does not mean that individual sin did not abound. But sin, ungodliness, and disrespect for God were not officially endorsed in education, government, and media. In fact, they were officially condemned and socially disapproved.

Speaking of the religious and moral conditions in America in 1784, Benjamin Franklin wrote:

Serious religion, under its various denominations, is not only tolerated, but respected and practised. Atheism is unknown there; Infidelity rare and secret; so that persons may live to a great age in that country without having their piety shocked by meeting with either an Atheist or an Infidel. And the Divine Being seems to have manifested his approbation of the mutual forbearance and kindness with which the different sects treat each other, by the remarkable prosperity with which he has been pleased to favor the whole country.[6]

Even Hollywood did not resort to profanity until the 1940s, and its assault on moral and family values did not occur until the sixties and seventies. Today, of course, murder in the guise of abortion and pornography in the name of freedom of the press are legalized by the highest court in the land. It is no wonder we are the crime and porno capital of the world.

Gradually, however, there is a fresh new spirit in the land. There is a new quest for "peace, quietness, morality, and reverence for God" in the hearts of our people. We are realizing that, unless a new breed of politician is elected to office, this nation will end up like Sodom and Gomorrah or Rome and Pompeii. That new breed of politician, regardless of political party, must be deeply committed to moral values. He must realize that this nation must have legislative reform. But to have legislative reform we must first have reformed legislators.

Everywhere I go, individuals confide that they are running for public office or praying about doing so. These are citizens who five years ago never gave thought to such a possibility. But the burden that God has placed on my heart during this past decade—reflected in my books, preaching, radio and television ministry, and the organization I lead in Washington, D.C.—is not mine alone. It is shared by thousands of other Christians, ministers, government workers, and fellow Americans. Before the nineties are through it will be shared by millions more—and we will have won the race for the 21st century!

An Unforgettable Experience

At 37,000 feet altitude my wife and I had a life-changing experience that explains the graphic change in our ministry.

For thirty years I had been a Bible-teaching pastor with a strong missionary-minded congregation. Together we had raised millions of dollars for foreign missions and had seen over 300 young people go into Christian work as ministers, missionaries, youth pastors, and Christian educators. Our church had given us sabbatical leave for one year after twenty years of service. So Bev and I offered ourselves free of charge to teach missionaries the family life principles which we had shared in our 600 Family Life Seminars. Forty-six countries and ten months later we were returning home to continue our ministry. So we were praying about how best to use our remaining years to serve our Lord.

As we thought about the honor we had just experienced of ministering to over one-sixth of the world's missionary force, it suddenly occurred to us that 85 percent of the world's missionaries were Americans! Eighty-five percent of the technology used by missionaries comes from America. A similar percentage of the money that supports world missions comes from this country.

God impressed us then that the most important thing we could do for the cause of Christ was to work for a moral, social, and spiritual revival for America—for a morally strong America provides God a powerful launching pad for the spread of the gospel worldwide. And since the last days of this century offer us incredible breakthroughs in high tech that can be incorporated into the spread of the gospel by dedicated well-trained and creative minds, a morally strong and religiously free America can reach untold billions of souls with the Word of God.

We had no idea Bev would found Concerned Women for America, the largest women's group in America. At this writing it numbers almost 600,000. Through "prayer and action," CWA is helping call America back to the religious heritage it was founded upon. Nor did I dream I would found the American Coalition for Traditional Values to help mobilize the 110,000 Bible-believing ministers of the nation to urge our government leaders to return this nation to traditional "one nation under God" values—or replace them with leaders who will.

We haven't done anything unusual. Like many other Christians and conservative activists, we have offered ourselves to God to serve Him and our country. It is my prayer that all who read this book will, like millions of Christians before us, offer their lives (including their time and talents), their fortunes, and their sacred honor to help win the race for the 21st century.

If we do, our children will one day rise up and call us blessed!

The End

For a free copy of the Tim LaHaye Capital Report and the Concerned Women for America Newsletter, write:

Dr. Tim LaHaye
P.O. Box 2700
Washington, D.C. 20013-2700

Discussion Questions

For Sunday school classes and small groups

Chapter One

1. Why is the end of the twentieth century called "the information age"?
2. What difference will the information age make to you? To your family?
3. How have computers revolutionized the manufacturing process? Telecommunications? Space travel?
4. Do you feel that a cashless society is desirable? Why? Why not?
5. How do you feel about all these technological changes and advances?

Chapter Two

1. How has future shock affected you? Your family? Your profession?
2. How can you minimize future shock's effect on you and your family?

3. What are some changes that will occur in the super-industrial revolution? What is The Third Wave?
4. How might the cottage industry affect your work? Your children's? What can you do to prepare yourself and your children for this megatrend?
5. What opportunity does the decentralization of authority give to Christians and the church?

Chapter Three

1. How does John Naisbitt predict the future? Does this give you any clues as to how you can be aware of coming trends?
2. What is the difference between short-term and long-term planning? Why has short-term planning failed America's businesses? How could short-term planning fail you and your family?
3. What is the difference between a democratic and a republican form of government? What form of government is the United States?
4. Do you believe that the two-party system is dead? Why or why not?
5. How can you and/or your church benefit from networking?

Chapter Four

1. What myths have kept Christians from influencing the twentieth century?
2. Do you agree with Dr. Jeffrey Hadden, who said, "The so-called Christian right, powered by TV evangelism, 'is destined to become the major social movement in America' during the late twentieth century"?
3. What is secular humanism? How did it influence education?
4. Which of the born-again movements has been most influential in your life? Why?
5. How can your church evangelize the community more effectively?

Chapter Five

1. What are the roots of the conservative movement? Trace its history from these roots to the election of President Reagan, noting

the milestones on a blackboard or flipchart.
2. What are the common beliefs of members of the conservative movement?
3. What is the New Right? Who are some of its members?
4. What was your opinion of conservatives before you read this chapter? What is it now?
5. Do you believe that our country will return to traditional values if the conservative trend continues? Why or why not?

Chapter Six

1. Do you believe that Christians should take an active part in the political process? Why or why not?
2. Can Christian political involvement make a difference to our country's future? Why or why not?
3. Do you believe that evangelical Christians should cooperate with other religious people to effect a return to moral values?
4. Is America a nation that has no room for God and His moral absolutes in its public policy, or is it a religious nation based on biblical principles? Why do you think so?
5. Should Christians hold 25 to 30 percent of public offices since we represent 25 to 30 percent of the population? Why or why not?

Chapter Seven

(If you have an attorney or judge in your congregation, you might ask him or her to be present for this discussion.)

1. Which of the conservative dreams for the future do you agree with? Why?
2. Which of the conservative dreams do you disagree with? Why?
3. How could individual Christians and the church work toward a spiritual revival in the last half of this century?
4. How could a freedom–with–responsibility philosophy be implemented by our judicial system?
5. How could a people-to-people food program be redirected to feed the hungry of the world?

Chapter Eight

1. How have the rights of parents been curtailed? How might they be curtailed in the future by a liberal government?
2. What changes in education are suggested by the quotation on page 143 from the article in _The Humanist_ magazine? By the quotation from Dr. Chester Pierce, a Harvard University professor?
3. What could happen to the electric church under a humanistic government?
4. What factors in the next decade will determine who will win the race for the 21st century?
5. How can you and members of your church influence your local government and your local educational system?

Chapter Nine

1. Why are United States manufacturers no longer competitive with foreign companies?
2. What are the three keys to holding a job in the future?
3. Look at the Changes in Key Industries chart on page 156 together. How will these changes affect you? How can you prepare your children for these changes?
4. Could you or someone else in your family begin a cottage industry? How?
5. Read 1 Corinthians 9:24–27, Galatians 5:22–23, and Colossians 3:16–17 together. What do these passages say about self-discipline? Does your work exemplify these standards?

Chapter Ten

1. What are the four types of families? How does your church minister to each of these families? How could you improve your ministry to the less traditional family types?
2. Which of Dr. LaHaye's suggestions would benefit your family most? Why? Make your goal for the next month to implement this suggestion.
3. Does your family have a TV policy? If so, what are your rules? If not, what rules might you set?
4. Which of Dr. LaHaye's financial suggestions appeals to you?

How could you implement it? Make this a goal for the coming
month.
5. How might you use your home for hospitality evangelism?

Chapter Eleven

(You might ask those in the church who work in the computer
industry or have extensive computer knowledge to attend this
meeting.)

1. How can our church utilize some of the new telecommunications technology? What equipment would be necessary?
2. What do you or your church do to encourage love, warmth, and
caring among members? What other things could you do?
3. What could you or your church do to assist members who are
out of work or need vocational guidance? What other things
could you or your church do?
4. What could your church do to minister to the poor in your city
or town?
5. How can your church help get out the vote for the 1988, 1990,
and 1992 elections?

Notes

Preface

1. Newt Gingrich, with David Drake and Marianne Gingrich, *Window of Opportunity: A Blueprint for the Future* (New York: Tom Doherty Associates, 1984), 11.

Chapter 1

1. Felicia Lee, "Expo Peeks into a Future Fantasyland," *USA Today,* April 18, 1985, A1.
2. Arthur Howe, "What's New in TV Sets? You Haven't Seen Anything Yet!" *The San Diego Union,* Nov. 4, 1984, D.
3. "Space Commercialization," *The San Diego Union,* Nov. 10, 1984, A6.
4. Walter Andrews, "Space Plane Held Possible," *The Washington Times,* April 2, 1985, A3.

Chapter 2

1. Alvin Toffler, *Previews & Premises* (New York: Bantam Books, 1983), 2.
2. Toffler, *Future Shock* (New York: Random House, 1970), 32.
3. Ibid., 165–166.
4. Ibid., 353–354.
5. Ibid., 357–358.
6. Ibid., 358.

7. Ibid., 384.
8. Ibid., 385.
9. Toffler, *The Third Wave* (New York: William Morrow & Company, 1980), 46–47.
10. Ibid., 47.
11. Ibid., 210.
12. Ibid., 213.
13. Ibid., 212–213.

Chapter 3

1. John Naisbitt, *Megatrends: Ten New Directions Transforming Our Lives* (New York: Warner Books, 1984), 12–14.
2. Ibid., 15.
3. Ibid., 5–6.
4. Ibid., 6.
5. Ibid., 7.
6. Ibid., 14.
7. Ibid., 36.
8. Ibid., 54.
9. Ibid., 55.
10. Ibid., 57.
11. Ibid., 58.
12. Ibid., 64.
13. Ibid., 79.
14. Ibid., 85.
15. Ibid.
16. Ibid., 91.
17. Ibid., 119.
18. Ibid., 121–123.
19. Ibid., 145.
20. Ibid., 175–176.
21. Ibid.
22. Ibid., 176–177.
23. Ibid., 178.
24. Ibid., 215.
25. Ibid.
26. Ibid., 226.
27. Ibid., 232.
28. Ibid., 259.
29. Ibid., 260.
30. Ibid., 261.

Chapter 4

1. John Lofton, "Advice from an Insider," *The Washington Times,* Feb. 24, 1986, D1.
2. George Gallup, Jr., and David Poling, *The Search For America's Faith* (Nashville: Abingdon, 1980), 44.

3. Ibid., 82.
4. Ibid., 79.
5. Ibid., 13.
6. Ibid., 18.
7. Rudolf Flesch, *Why Johnny Still Can't Read* (New York: Harper & Row, 1981), 1,2.
8. "40% of Viewers Watch TV Preachers," *The Washington Post,* Nov. 2, 1985, H10.

Chapter 5

1. *Facts and Figures on Government Finance* (Washington: Tax Foundation, Incorporated, 1983), 99.
2 Richard A. Viguerie, *The New Right: We're Ready To Lead* (The Viguerie Company, 1981), 41–43.

Chapter 6

1. "Feminism," *Time,* Sept. 2, 1985, 57.
2. David E. Rosenbaum, "A Good Election for Poll Takers," *The New York Times,* Nov. 8, 1984, A19.
3. "Religion in America, 50 Years: 1935–1985," *The Gallup Report,* Report No. 236, May 1985, 38.
4. "40% of Viewers Watch TV Preachers," *The Washington Post,* Nov. 1985, H10.
5. Ibid.
6. For a legal opinion on this subject and brochure "What a Church Can and Cannot Do," write American Coalition for Traditional Values, 122 "C" Street NW, Suite 850, Washington, D.C. 20001.
7. George Washington, Farewell Address, Sept. 19, 1796.
8. John Adams, Address to the Militia of Massachusetts, 1798.

Chapter 7

1. Vern McLellan, *Christians in the Political Arena* (Charlotte, N.C.: Associates, 1986).
2. J. Peter Grace, *The President's Private Sector Survey on Cost Control,* Vol. I, 4,5.
3. *The World Almanac and Book of Facts 1986* (New York: Newspaper Enterprise Association, 1986), 99.
4. James McKeever, *The AIDS Plague* (Medford, Oregon: Omega Publications, 1986), 53,54.
5. "Herpes can be passed to others even if there are no symptoms." *The Washington Times,* June 12, 1986, D2.
6. "Children Having Children," *Time,* Dec. 9, 1985, 79.
7. John A. Stormer, *The Death of a Nation* (Florissant, Missouri: The Liberty Bell Press, 1968), 129–131.
8. Ibid.
9. Ibid.

Chapter 8

1. Gloria Steinem, *Michigan Free Press,* April 15, 1974.

2. Gloria Steinem, *Saturday Review of Education,* March 1973.
3. Nanci Hellmich, "Casual Sex: Hot '60s, Chilly '80s," *USA Today,* Feb. 19, 1986, D2.
4. Ibid.
5. "Spread of AIDS may send sex mores back to the '50s," *The Washington Times,* April 21, 1986.
6. Ibid.
7. John J. Dunphy, "A Religion For A New Age," *The Humanist* (January/February 1983) 26.
8. Harold G. Shane & June Grant Shane, "Forecast For The Seventies," *Today's Education, The NEA Journal* (January 1969), 31.
9. Dr. Chester Pierce made this statement in his keynote address at the Association for Childhood Education International (ACEI) Annual Study Conference held at Denver, Colorado, in April 1972. Dr. Pierce is Professor of Education and Psychiatry in the faculty of Medicine and Graduate School of Education, Harvard University.
10. For more information about such training write to American Coalition for Traditional Values, 122 "C" Street N.W., Suite 850, Washington, D.C. 20001.

Chapter 9

1. Lucia Solorzano, "How Schools Train Kids For Tomorrow's Jobs," *U.S. News and World Report,* Dec. 23, 1985, 47.
2. John Naisbitt, *Megatrends* (New York: Warner Books, 1984), 23.
3. Newt Gingrich, *Window of Opportunity,* (New York: Tom Doherty Associates, 1984), 2–3.
4. Adapted from Monroe W. Karmin, "Jobs of the Future," *U.S. News & World Report,* Dec. 23, 1985, 40.

Chapter 11

1. "Religion in America," *The Gallup Report,* Report No. 236, May 1985, 40, 42, 47, 50.
2. Ibid., 51.
3. "Morality," *U.S. News and World Report,* Dec. 9, 1985, 52.
4. Claudia Wallis, "Children Having Children," *Time,* Dec. 9, 1985, 79.
5. "Gallup Poll," *Newsweek,* March 18, 1985, 60.
6. George D. Youstry, *America in Person* (Bob Jones University Press, Inc., 1975), 105. (Written by Benjamin Franklin while living in France, just after the conclusion of the treaty of peace with Great Britain, which he had helped to negotiate, and published in London as "Information to Those Who Would Remove to America.")

LaHaye
Temperament
Analysis

- a test to identify your primary and secondary temperaments
- a description of your predominant characteristics
- information regarding your vocational aptitudes and possible vocations suited to you
- recommendations on improving your work habits
- a list of your spiritual gifts, in the order of their priority
- suggestions for where you can best serve in your church
- steps for overcoming your ten greatest weaknesses
- counsel on marital adjustment and parental leadership
- special advice to singles, divorcees, pastors, and the widowed

Your personal 13-to 16-page evaluation letter from Dr. Tim LaHaye will be permanently bound in a handsome vinyl leather portfolio.

... your opportunity
to know yourself
better!